Marriage in Black

Despite the messages we hear from social scientists, policymakers, and the media, black Americans do in fact get married—and many of these marriages last for decades. *Marriage in Black* offers a progressive perspective on black marriage that rejects talk of black relationship "pathology" in order to provide an understanding of enduring black marriage that is richly lived. The authors offer an in-depth investigation of details and contexts of black married life, and seek to empower black married couples whose intimate relationships run contrary to common—but often inaccurate—stereotypes. Considering historical influences from Antebellum slavery onward, this book investigates contemporary married life among more than 60 couples born after the passage of the Civil Rights Act. Husbands and wives tell their stories, from how they met, to how they decided to marry, to what their life is like five years after the wedding and beyond. Their stories reveal the experiences of the American-born and of black immigrants from Africa or the Caribbean, with explorations of the "ideal" marriage, parenting, finances, work, conflict, the criminal justice system, religion, and race. These couples show us that black family life has richness that belies common stereotypes, with substantial variation in couples' experiences based on social class, country of origin, gender, religiosity, and family characteristics.

Katrina Bell McDonald earned her PhD in Sociology from the University of California at Davis. She is Associate Professor of Sociology, Co-Director of the Center for Africana Studies at the Johns Hopkins University, and an Associate of the Hopkins Population Center. She joined the faculty in 1994 and teaches and conducts research on the African-American family, race and racism, racial privilege, intersectionality, and qualitative research methods. She has been happily married for 23 years.

Caitlin Cross-Barnet earned her PhD in Sociology from the Johns Hopkins University in 2010. She is a sociologist, public health researcher, and an Associate of the Hopkins Population Center. Her current research focuses on the social determinants of health. She has taught courses on research methods, public health, gender, race-ethnicity, and social inequality. She has been happily married for 26 years.

Given all the negative things written about marriage among blacks, it is refreshing—even inspiring—to read the stories of successful black married couples and to learn how they make their marriages work.

Andrew Cherlin, *Benjamin H. Griswold III Professor of Public Policy and Chair of the Sociology Department, Johns Hopkins University; Author of* The Marriage Go-Round: The State of Marriage and Family in America Today

Marriage in Black is a comprehensive empirical examination of marriage among African Americans, including topics ranging from marriage patterns and attitudes to gender relations, childrearing, and conflict resolution. The authors use a multiethnic feminist perspective to analyze interviews from a class- and race- diverse group of native-born African Americans, Black immigrants, and White married couples. The voices of these couples provide a framework for engaging and critiquing an array of sociological theories on marriage and family life. Situating each topic within the context of historic and current laws and social policies that continue to malign and marginalize African-American marriages, Katrina Bell McDonald and Caitlin Cross-Barnet effectively challenge the social deficit perspective on black married life and rectify the scholarly neglect of the topic. By examining intraracial differences among Blacks, the book answers the call for a more nuanced portrait of family life among people of African ancestry and emphasizes the intersection between cultural and structural forces that shape their lives. This book offers a refreshing reprieve from the litany of research focusing on the marriage decline among African Americans.

Shirley A. Hill, *Professor Emeritus of Sociology; Past President of Sociologists for Women in Society*

Many have researched the marriage gap between white and black couples, but little attention has been paid to the black marriages that do form, and how they might be distinct from other marriages. Katrina Bell McDonald and Caitlin Cross-Barnet fill this gap and present a compelling sociological analysis of contemporary Black marriages in America. Drawing upon in-depth interviews with African-Americans born in the U.S., black immigrants from Africa and the Caribbean, and white

American couples, this book demonstrates the rich diversity among black marriages in America, distinct features of these relationships, and the historical and continuing impact of race relations in America on black marriages. A must-read for any graduate student studying marriage or race!

Arielle Kuperberg, *PhD., Associate Professor and Director of Undergraduate Studies in Sociology, University of North Carolina at Greensboro*

McDonald and Cross-Barnet accomplish the heroic task of contradicting current stereotypes about marriage in the American black community, They show conclusively, through vibrant vignettes from interviews with 60 couples, most of them black and all of them married for at least 5 years, that there is substantial support for the idea of being married, and that many contemporary black couples are in long-term, stable marriages in which they have varied ideas about friendship, love and passion, parenting, and egalitarian relationships. By interviewing some who came to the U.S. from Africa or the Caribbean and others born in the U.S., they show us how unproductive it has been to treat black couples as a homogenous group. A must-read for all who want to understand contemporary black marriages in America.

Philip A. Cowan, *Professor of Psychology Emeritus, University of California, Berkeley;*
Carolyn Pape Cowan, *Adjunct Professor of Psychology, Emerita, University of California, Berkeley*

Katrina Bell McDonald and Cross-Barnet tackle the breath of complex issues in contemporary married life—childrearing, sex, money, religion—and while this is the usual array of topics one might find in a magazine article, unlike the magazines, the authors never lost sight of the fact that this is a serious piece of research. The analysis brings new understanding of how African descendants in the U.S. navigate the history of forced separation, structural impediments and countervailing cultural norms to exhibit through their very existence that marriage is—indeed—"for black people."

Thomas A. LaVeist, *PhD, Chairman and Professor, The George Washington University*

Marriage in Black

The Pursuit of Married Life among
American-born and Immigrant Blacks

**Katrina Bell McDonald and
Caitlin Cross-Barnet**

Routledge
Taylor & Francis Group

NEW YORK AND LONDON

First published 2018
by Routledge
711 Third Avenue, New York, NY 10017

and by Routledge
2 Park Square, Milton Park, Abingdon, Oxon OX14 4RN

Routledge is an imprint of the Taylor & Francis Group, an informa business

© 2018 Taylor & Francis

Library of Congress Cataloging-in-Publication Data
A catalog record for this book has been requested

ISBN: 978-1-138-49765-8 (hbk)
ISBN: 978-1-138-49767-2 (pbk)
ISBN: 978-1-351-01818-0 (ebk)

Typeset in Bembo
by Deanta Global Publishing Services, Chennai, India

To our families, who inspire us to do our part in bringing black marriage and family, in all of its configurations, in from the margins:

To Ray, Jordan, David, Sharon, Little David, Kameron, and Kerri McDonald

To Mike, Emily, Joshua, and Ezekiel "Story" Cross-Barnet

CONTENTS

ACKNOWLEDGMENTS

It takes a village to write a book. We wish to express our gratitude for funding we received from the American Sociological Association's Fund to Advance the Discipline; the Horowitz Foundation for Social Policy; the Program for the Study of Women, Gender and Sexuality; the Center for Africana Studies at the Johns Hopkins University; and the Hopkins Population Center.

We received intellectual and personal support from so many of our colleagues at Johns Hopkins and elsewhere that they are too numerous to mention all by name, but special thanks go to Andrew J. Cherlin, Emily Agree, and Beverly Silver of Johns Hopkins; Floyd Hayes, former senior lecturer at the Center for Africana Studies; and Pamela Bennett of the University of Maryland, Baltimore County.

Many graduate students worked in research assistantships or offered research support by notetaking during interviews, transcribing, compiling and organizing data, coding, and conducting analyses. We offer special thanks to Nazish Zafar, Sika Koudou, Elizabeth Talbert, and Kiara Nerenberg. We were also fortunate to have assistance from many undergraduates at Johns Hopkins over the years. We are grateful to them all, but especially Sean Thompson.

We thank Ellen Kliman for her impeccable transcriptions.

We thank the editors and anonymous referees of Routledge Press for their helpful reviews and other feedback.

Some of the substance of this book was presented at conferences, including those of the Southern Sociological Society, the Eastern Sociological Society, and the American Sociological Association, and in the journal *Societies*.

There is no better way to learn the joys and challenges of marriage than being in one—to a legal spouse or a writing partner. From Katrina: I am so grateful that I was supported by not only my loving husband, Ray, and my devoted son, Jordan, but by a host of sister-friends and extended kin who always knew what to say when the journey of writing this book got rough. Caitlin has been a long-time friend who I always knew would make a wonderful writing partner. We went through much together as wives and I look forward to many more years of spending our professional and personal lives side by side.

From Caitlin: I offer my deepest gratitude to Michael Cross-Barnet, my partner in everything, who financially supported our family so that I could earn a PhD, spent countless evenings along with our three children while I ran off to conduct interviews, and never lost faith as I spent years wading in data to tell the stories of the couples Katrina and I met. Mike also read and edited the final text. Katrina has been my mentor and friend for more than a decade now. When I entered graduate school with three young children in tow, she was the only member of the department who was also raising a child. We bonded over the trials and tribulations of marriage and motherhood as much as a passion for sociology and qualitative research.

Finally, we both offer our deepest and most sincere thanks to the couples who gave us their time and let us into the most personal relationship of their lives.

THE SOCIO-HISTORICAL UNSHACKLING OF AFRICAN-AMERICAN RELATIONSHIPS

Marvin and Jennifer Johnson, an American-born black couple, met at a local college, where they both studied areas of social work and justice. They now have three healthy daughters, and Jennifer is pregnant again with a boy. They have just a bought a new house in the city where they can raise their growing family. Although they fought frequently before they married, Jennifer said, "It just feels like God has moved in our marriage." Now they rarely argue. Jennifer believes female submission is essential to a successful marriage, and that women prioritizing work or school over family responsibilities are selfish. She said that black women in particular need to give up the role of the "power woman." Jennifer runs a small business from their home and occasionally takes a substitute teaching shift, but Marvin is the primary breadwinner, working two jobs. While Jennifer extolled submission, Marvin spoke of their marriage as a partnership and said it is important for spouses to have an equal role in everything. Jennifer agreed that "we always end up coming together" on resolving problems and making decisions. Especially now that Jennifer is at the end of her pregnancy, Marvin cleans, does laundry, bathes the children, and goes shopping, and said he loves doing it. Marvin said, "I wouldn't trade being married to Jennifer and raising a family together for anything in the world."

When Anthony and Ava Tompkins first met, Ava said, God told her that Anthony was to be her husband. Now, married for about eight years and raising two daughters in a spacious house in the suburbs, the Tompkins said that marriage has gotten better every year since the wedding.

Ava, born and raised in Bermuda, remains devoted to "family first." Anthony, who has Caribbean parents but was born and raised in the United States, agreed he was self-centered in the early years, but he has come to embrace Ava's family values, especially now that they are parents. He believes they play similar roles in the marriage and that's how it should be. His younger daughter attends daycare at the university where he coaches, and he picks up his older daughter from school on his way home. Ava, who arrives home first and cooks dinner, believes in traditional roles for women in general, but not for herself. She loves her job teaching high school, and she loves being the family's primary breadwinner. "If Anthony makes more, I'm like, I will make more," she said. "I will fight hard to make more." When it comes to marriage, she said, "My ideal is the man should lead," then added, "[but] I'm to be his advisor if there's a decision to be made. I'm there to give my opinion whether it's wanted or not."

Danny and Alena Chebet met at their church in Kenya when Alena was 17 years old, five years before their marriage. Under pressure from their families, the two married about six months after their first child was born and soon after Alena finished college. Two more children followed. Alena explained that children complete their marital picture and help with the "gloomy days"; there is a strong sense that their marriage is inseparable from the children and their parenting roles. They moved to the United States, where Danny had family members and where he felt he could pursue his dreams. Alena has her master's and a steady income, but Danny's work schedule and income fluctuate. He tries to work more so that he will earn more than Alena. Danny said that if they had remained in Kenya, there would be a lot of family pressure for Alena not to work, and he thinks this would be unpleasant. He does, however, wish that she could stay home in the United States so that she could raise their children with better "moral values" that those he sees in American families. Alena said that she tends to have more of an ideal regarding marriage. She thinks more in terms of "don'ts" and sometimes compares Danny to her father, whose authoritarian marriage style she did not like: "I want to have some say in getting that final word."

Andrew and Michelle Waller, a white couple, laugh at couples with traditional values and see the average marriage as boring and routine. Michelle works the night shift three days a week as a nurse for an inner-city hospital. Andrew does bookkeeping full time and is taking classes to advance his career. Michelle became pregnant shortly after they met. Neither had *attended college when they married, and their older daughter was born shortly after their wedding, when Michelle was 19 and Andrew was 20. Their second daughter was born four years later. Michelle wanted to be home with the girls when they were small, and Andrew was worried when she began nursing school that she would no longer need him as a provider. They earn similar incomes now even though Michelle does not work full-time, and they were able to purchase a tiny, well-kept house outside the city. Although they profess to split responsibilities in half, Michelle seems to do the bulk of the cooking, cleaning, and management of the girls' lives; Andrew talked about grilling. Andrew is focused on increasing his earning power so that Michelle will not bring in the bigger paycheck when she switches to full-time work in the next couple of years. They said they fight a lot—it's in their "nature"—and often don't see each other for days at a time because of their work schedules. At the same time, they agreed that they are each other's best friend and would never leave each other because they are very happy.*

This will not be your typical journey through the analysis of dismal statistics on the status of black[1] marriages in America. Neither will it be a purely celebratory tale steeped in Afrocentrism that ignores what underlies black marital trends, especially the trends of non-marriage and divorce. There is no denying that black married couples are at greater risk of divorce than couples from other racial-ethnic groups[2] and that currently only about 31% of blacks are married (versus 48% for Hispanics and 55% for whites).[3] It is also a fact, however, that black marriage has survived—through the transatlantic slave trade, Reconstruction, lynching, political disenfranchisement, and fierce racial segregation that persists to the present day in the United States. And despite all of these barriers, blacks are just as intent as other groups on marrying at some point in their lives.[4] The black couples introduced above offer the kind of heterosexual marriage stories we seek to illuminate.

We wish to flip the script. Virtually all discussions of contemporary black heterosexual marriage focus on the failure to marry, the negative consequences of relationship instability, or marital dissolution. The literature explores such subjects as why black women choose single motherhood, why black fathers do not stick around for the long haul, why black couples who cohabit don't marry, and how extended kin networks operate in lieu of the nuclear family arrangement and with less success. *Numerous examples of such research and commentary abound.*[5] In 2001, Bachand and Caron wrote, "[w]hile an abundance of literature exists on the marital relationship, most focuses on divorce and the consequences of divorce in our society" (161);[6] this is all the more true in literature that considers black marriages. The intense focus on difficulties in getting or staying married has precluded direct investigation into determining what may provide for black marital longevity or for black marital content- ment. This leaves us with a limited understanding of the world of black marriage and desensitizes us to the world of black couples who remain married despite their struggles. Thus, *Marriage in Black* contributes to a shift in sociological research towards examining contemporary black marriages currently in place.

Public policy has been focused on promoting "healthy" marriage, beginning with the enactment of the 1996 welfare reform law,[7] a law directed largely at poor black women. Child outcomes have often been central to considering the health of black marriages, though the focus is most commonly on how parents negatively impact the health and welfare of their children.[8] Despite the interest in promoting marriage among black Americans, definitions of healthy marriage have not con- sidered that the concept of marital "health" may not be universal. There has been little attention given to the diversity of black marital life, pri- marily because few scholars acknowledge the diversity of black origins and black experience in the United States, neglecting immigration, inte- gration, and inequality within the black population.[9] Much of this is due to an abundance of scholarship on marriage across socioeconomic or class lines where poverty and child outcomes tend to take a front seat.[10] In almost all of these cases, blacks are generally treated as a monolithic cultural population.

So, in this book we make an attempt at balance—a vision of contem- porary, heterosexual black marital life that ebbs and flows. We proceed from the progressive perspective on black marriage that suggests that we would do best to move away from talk of black relationship "pathology" in order to offer greater understanding of how personal decisions and structural social forces can lead to black marriage that is richly lived.

We strongly argue that the experience of black marriage is not only culturally different from marriages among other racial-ethnic groups in America, but also among black couples with different ethnic origins. Blacks are most commonly discussed as though they are a homogenous racial mass with no variation in ethnic and cultural substance. Yet historical and contemporary immigration patterns dictate that the study of black marital life in the United States must at least incorporate those African- and Caribbean-born, the two largest black immigrant groups in the United States. Recent migration from Africa has resulted in the fastest growth in the African-born population of the United States in the past four decades.[11] According to the *New York Times*, "more (Africans) have arrived voluntarily than the total who disembarked in chains before the United States outlawed international slave trafficking in 1807."[12] Still, half of black immigrants hail from the countries of the Caribbean.[13]

Demographic changes in African-American marriage and in black immigration to the United States have been accompanied by dramatic changes in American attitudes and social norms regarding gender and marriage. For example, sociologists of the family place great emphasis on gender relations and on how men and women negotiate prescribed social roles within marriage. Beginning in the 1970s, the sharp increase in women's paid labor force participation led to a societal rethinking of family gender lines. While black and white married women now engage in paid work at roughly equal rates, this shift in the rate of employment represented substantially more change for white wives than for black women, who historically had been much more likely to be employed.[14] As such, the debate about the gendered balance between paid employment and unpaid home-based labor was new in the context of white, middle-class life, but perhaps less so in the context of black family life. For white women, stepping into the workforce was sometimes seen as a step toward egalitarianism. This 1970s shift also had more enduring consequences for black men, who were more likely than white men to have blue collar jobs. The historical differences in the necessity and prevalence of dual-earner households may have driven speculation that black families have held egalitarian beliefs for a long time. With women now contributing a much larger portion of the family income than in the past, black women even more so than white women,[15] feminists and feminist scholars question the assumption that women will continue to enact gender-based family roles.[16] The "second shift" that women have endured—engaging in two full-time jobs, first at work and then at home—demonstrated that patriarchal hegemony was alive and well.[17] Unfortunately, there is no analysis of the position of Black women of the "second shift" in this earlier scholarship. And since African and Caribbean[18] families have primarily been studied in their countries of origin or countries other than the United States, and with a focus other than gender relations, there is little in the current literature that explores the context of Black immigrant life in regard to gender and marriage at all.

Interest in *egalitarianism* spans at least the past two centuries in our nation. It is best embodied in the civil rights era, which focused on equality of the races, of the sexes, and later of gays, lesbians, and other sexual minorities. In this work, we are particularly interested in the continued struggle to change gender attitudes and social norms, a struggle that began in earnest in the mid-1900s. Researchers have at times examined the phenomenon of men and women experimenting with egalitarianism as an alternative to the oppressive traditional marriage structure. At least one economic historian, Robert William Fogel,[19] predicts that the 1950s mythical version of traditional family is likely to become a stronger rather than a weaker image in this postmodern era due to new media and new technology allowing for and putting greater emphasis on workplace family connections. That is, he believes that the weakening on the private/public will allow for a stronger desire of family closeness.

About eight years ago, we asked our colleague, the distinguished sociologist Andrew J. Cherlin (Benjamin H. Griswold III Professor of Public Policy at Johns Hopkins), the question of whether sociologists had proven that egalitarian marriage was better than non-egalitarian marriage back in the 1960s and 1970s. He responded, somewhat surprised and unsatisfied, "No, I really don't think we did." So we set out to write *Marriage in Black*, not just to revive the debate on egalitarian marriage, but to make sure Black families were properly at the table. Even though a qualitative study cannot offer definitive conclusions on this, we were determined to make egalitarianism the centerpiece of our text and use our data to reveal the various ways that couples speak of egalitarianism (if at all) and the ways they attempt to adopt it in their relationships.

Despite decades of research and discussion, there is little consensus as to what constitutes egalitarian marriage. Definitions range from equality of spousal earning power, to shared "final word" decision-making, to sharing of household duties, to equal contributions of nurturance, to equivalent well-being, and to comparable amount of work versus leisure time.[20] It is said that, "A true egalitarian would neither disapprove of a woman assuming the male role of business executive nor disapprove of a man assuming the stereotypically female role of child care provider" (72).[21] Better still, Brighouse and Wright state that "strong egalitarianism" is

> a structure of social relations in which the division of labor around housework and caregiving within the family and occupational distributions within the public sphere are unaffected by gender. By "unaffected by gender," we mean that there would be no socially constructed gender-differentiated norms around the division of labor: no specific activities would be thought of as men's work or women's work; nor would any activities be seen as more appropriate for men or for women.[22] (363)

Recent studies indicate that the majority of young couples believe in egalitarian relationships between men and women in marriage,[23] marking the relevant generational shift serving as the foundation of the research reported here. Whether this shift is equally relevant for black and white Americans remains unclear, thus our interest in at least exploring qualitatively the extent to which this ideal is expressed among the couples we interviewed.

Changes in gender attitudes and social norms have focused to date primarily on white, middle-class patterns of marital life. Thus, very little is known about how egalitarianism varies among racial/cultural groups in either contemporary or historical contexts, but many scholars have posited that deep African cultural roots, the historical legacy of slavery, and economic conditions resulting from ongoing racism and discrimination have led to different marital ideals and practices for *black* couples. Robert Staples and Leanor Johnson, for example, have posited that,

> [u]nlike the White family, which is typically believed to be patriarchal and sustained by the economic dependence of women [on men], the Black dyad has been characterized by more egalitarian roles and economic parity in North America ... [and] relationships between the [Black] genders were ordered along sociopsychological dimensions rather than reflecting an economic compulsion to marry and sustain marriage.[24] (153)

Still, research indicates that while African-American men are more positive than white men about women's workforce participation, on other attitudes regarding gender and marriage African-American men are more conservative or "traditional" than white men.[25] So while there are oft-repeated claims and speculation in the sociological and feminist literature of egalitarianism among blacks,[26] there has been little substantiation.

And so, *Marriage in Black* is largely about the ideals heterosexual black couples hold for themselves in marriage, particularly where gender relations are concerned. But it is also a rare glimpse into what every-day black marriage truly looks like. Not like a sitcom. Not like a reality show. And not like most Hollywood films. You will see that black couples are not trivial or arbitrary in the construction of their lives. Here, husbands and wives, along with their children and parents, and their extended and cultural kin, work to hold marriages together for the long-haul. Each holds a marital ideology, a vision of what they believe it means to be married and how to make marriage work. Black couples struggle, like couples of all backgrounds, to structure marriage so as to satisfy and survive. And these couples are by no means a homogeneous population; while from similar national and cultural roots, the various black cultures represented here exhibit important differences in their approach to housework, money and finances, sexual relations, family health, childbearing and parenting, religion, and gender relations. And we find that it is marital ideology in regard to gender relations that seems to flavor virtually all else that must be managed by the couples, American-born and immigrant.

Black Immigration and Assimilation

> Odell and Kylie Velarde miss many things about their home country. There, they said, their toddler could play in the streets under the watchful eye of family members and extended kin. No one seemed perplexed by their difference in skin color—but in the United States when Kylie travels with her daughter, other black women constantly ask if her husband is white. She has had to learn racial terminology that her American counterparts do not find offensive. Like many couples who hail from the Caribbean, Odell and Kylie were together for many years before formalizing their union, and Kylie is pleased that Odell, who is fifteen years her senior, had mostly lost interest in pursuing other women by the time they met. She believes his only infidelity was during her pregnancy, and she finds this acceptable because he did not give her a sexually transmitted infection. Both Odell and Kylie are well educated and have years of work experience in STEM fields, but these skills have not transferred to the job market in the United States, where Odell works as a laborer and Kylie is a hotel maid. Despite the drudgery of low-wage work, the couple feels they have great economic opportunity in the United States. Most important to them, though they now live in a small apartment, they no longer have to share a home with Kylie's extended family. They miss things about their original home, but they have committed to a life in the United States.

Forty-five percent of the couples whose experiences are reported from this study are immigrant couples, from either the continent of African or the Caribbean. The process of assimilating after immigration to America may seem to some like a simple process, but it can be taxing in a number of ways. First, assimilation generally means "the process through which individuals and groups of differing heritages acquire the basic habits, attitudes, and mode of life of an embracing culture."[27] In this case, assimilation is a process that considers to what extent immigrants take on the values and behavior patterns of the dominant American culture,[28] with "dominant" meaning white America or "mainstream" America. It is often considered a straight-line process during which the "melting pot" absorbs immigrants until they become integral to the dominant culture. But such "melting" did not occur at the same rate or with same result for all groups. This is particularly true for African Americans, despite their long history of residence in the United States. In the 1960s—hundreds of years after their forced immigration into enslavement, 100 years after the end of the Civil War, and through the ratification of the Civil Rights Amendment—Milton Gordon posited that African Americans had only undergone a very mild version of assimilation (76).

While most immigrants come to the United States voluntarily to seek opportunity, and others come as refugees, escaping dire circumstances such as war, most American-born blacks' ancestors came to the United States involuntarily as part of the slave trade. The vast majority came directly from West Africa, but some were initially routed through the Caribbean during the slave era, some imported to the United States mainland as slaves, but others arriving as free people.[29] Ogbu and Simons[30] point out that "involuntary minorities" have been made a part of American society against their own will. Black involuntary minorities are further disadvantaged in the United States as caste-like minorities, meaning that by virtue of their origins in Africa, their relatively low social status, and their dark skin, they are perpetually locked into a lower group status that is even more confining than being locked into a lower social class.[31] Thus, although most blacks can trace their American residency back much further than even some whites can, they still occupy an "outsider" position in relation to the dominant culture, much as many immigrants initially do.

American Immigration Policy

Early immigration laws were designed to maintain the dominant status of whites, particularly those who were educated and hailed from Western Europe. As sociologist Stephen Klineberg notes,

> The law was just unbelievable in its clarity of racism. It declared that Northern Europeans are a superior subspecies of the white race. The Nordics were superior to the Alpines, who in turn were superior to the Mediterranean peoples, and all of them were superior to the Jews and the Asians.[32]

Significant immigration laws were enacted in 1917, 1924 (the Johnson Reed Act), and 1952 (the McCarran-Walter Bill). The McCarran-Walter Bill reorganized the structure of immigration law but kept quotas intended to preserve the majority status of whites.[33] During this period, limited numbers of immigrants from the Caribbean, primarily skilled workers and educated professionals, most of whom were black, continued to arrive, but immigration from Africa to the United States was almost non-existent.

During the era of racially restricted immigration, assimilation was about blacks unlearning their "inferior culture." However, this societal goal and the attitudes surrounding it began to break down as the Civil Rights Movement gained strength. The Civil Rights Act of 1964 set the stage for change in immigration policy, as the end to legalized discrimination based on race, color, religion, or national origin was not compatible with the immigration quota systems still in place. Potential for increasing minority racial and ethnic groups' assimilation was reinforced by laws and court decisions that followed, such as the Voting Rights Act of 1965, which removed barriers such as literacy tests and poll taxes that had kept most blacks in the South from voting, and the Supreme Court decision *Loving vs. Virginia* in 1967, which made it unconstitutional to prohibit interracial marriage.[34]

The Immigration and Naturalization Act (or Hart-Celler Act), signed by President Lyndon Johnson in 1965, abolished the national-origin quotas put in place earlier and set the stage for a new wave of voluntary black immigrants. In particular, it prioritized family reunification. The act also opened up immigration from the Caribbean Islands.[35] Initially after this act was passed, black immigrants hailed primarily from the Caribbean, which had maintained a limited stream of immigrants even under the restrictive policies before 1965. Black Africans, primarily from sub-Saharan Africa, began arriving in the late 1970s, hailing primarily from Nigeria, Ethiopia, Kenya, Ghana, and Somalia.[36] While there were a small number of black immigrants from Africa and the Caribbean who arrived in the United States as refugees, most were voluntary immigrants.[37]

Black Immigration Processes and Outcomes

Structural forces rooted in racial oppression have prevented full integration of blacks into the dominant society in the United States. Some argue that these structural barriers feed directly and indirectly from blacks being forcibly separated from their African homeland. Sociologist Ira De

Augustine Reid noted in his 1939 book, *The Negro Immigrant*,[38] that immigration caused a fundamental breach from the African homeland, leading to significant changes in the way in which blacks lived their lives.

Life in Caribbean society followed a very different path than in the United States before and after slavery, with black Caribbeans becoming a majority in those lands and with racism as it existed being less institutionalized. Contemporary black African and Caribbean immigrants generally come from countries of origin where the vast majority of residents are also black, and arrive seeking opportunities for employment and education. African immigrants arrive with no historical burden of forced migration. These different patterns of entry into United States society demonstrate that perceptions of black Americans as a singular ethnic or cultural entity are fundamentally inaccurate.

Despite the different paths leading to African-descended peoples' settlement in the United States, assimilating (even among those blacks with long histories in the United States) continues to be complicated by racism, both overt and structural. Scholars such as Portes and Zhou[39] and Ogbu and Simons[40] suggest that the way blacks settle in housing, work, school, and economic security can sometimes resemble the white middle class *or* the black "underclass." Either means shedding the home culture's values and customs. Some blacks arrive in this country bent on not experiencing downward assimilation toward the class status of poor American-born blacks, a status that is plagued by negative stereotypes and a history of American racism.[41] Others, given these same facts, feel a strong solidarity with all blacks from the start.[42] Tension generally arises among veteran and newly arrived blacks, who each feel the other has an attitude of superiority and distance themselves from the other, hoping for greater acceptance by the mainstream.[43] These tensions are the unsettling vestiges of American race-based slavery.

Black Immigrant Marriage Trends

On the whole, African and Caribbean immigrants are notably different from American-born blacks and from each other in their marriage patterns and practices. For example, black immigrants are far more likely to be married than American-born blacks, with marriage rates more comparable to those of whites.[44] Black immigrants are less likely to marry whites than are American-born Blacks.[45] Black Caribbeans have marriage expectations that differ from that of American-born blacks, with American-born black women having lower expectations of marrying and black Caribbeans' expectations of marrying tied to whether they are currently in a relationship and have children with their partner.[46] African immigrants are more likely to be married and their children are more likely to live in a two-parent household than Caribbean immigrants.[47] Some African immigrants come from areas of the continent that sanction polygamy,[48] though polygamy is not recognized or legal in the United States. Still, some believe that the long history of polygamy among some blacks might be reflected in families from both Africa and the Caribbean, who often have a more collective orientation than American families, with extended family relationships that are less common among the American-born, who are more likely to value the nuclear family.

Expectations of how marriage should be organized and practiced also differ among groups. Caribbean families are often thought to be matrifocal, with women running households and raising children with limited input from their husbands.[49] In the Caribbean, this is accompanied by high rates of family formation outside of marriage, with many marriages that begin as common law unions becoming formal years later. At the same time, Caribbean culture is highly patriarchal, and marriages have often included limits on women's independence and a tolerance for domestic violence and men's infidelity.[50] Gender roles are strictly defined in Caribbean culture, and after immigrating, women are often still expected to adhere to traditional values.[51] While childless wives do not have high status in many sub-Saharan African cultures, motherhood is exalted.[52] Still, household decision making in most African countries is usually dominated by men, and couples must make significant adjustments if they wish to adopt more American gender roles once in the United States.

A Few Words on Social Class

As we indicated earlier, the study of black life often goes hand in hand with the study of poverty. There are some studies that chronicle middle-class black life,[53] but for the most part, being black in American is associated with being poor. That is ridiculous, of course. Poverty rates among black Americans may be more than double what they are among whites, but more than 75% of black Americans are *not* poor, and black families span the same class range found among any other racial-ethnic group. That is not to say that longstanding structural discrimination hasn't influenced black Americans' ability to move up the class ladder and recognize the American Dream. Housing discrimination, unfair lending policies, segregated and unequal education, and wage discrimination have made it difficult for black families to build wealth over generations. Today, even black families with high incomes often have less wealth than lower-income white families.[54] But disadvantage relative to whites is not the same as universal poverty.

Like definitions of egalitarianism, definitions of class vary far and wide. Beginning with business ownership and the ability to earn money on the backs of workers, class definitions grew to include social status and political power, income, white collar vs. blue collar work for men, wealth and property ownership, and education level.[55] We constructed a social class matrix that considered home ownership and neighborhood quality, employment status, income levels and stability, and education to define social class among our couples. Most couples in which spouses are college educated or work in white collar jobs also have sufficient income and own their own homes—these couples make up the bulk of our middle-class couples. Couples in which spouses completed high school but have little or no college education and work in blue- or pink-collar jobs sometimes owned their own homes, but their houses were often smaller and in neighborhoods that were somewhat run down. Sometimes their employment was tenuous, but they could usually make ends meet. These were our working-class couples. Couples who hadn't finished high school, lived hand to mouth, and regularly dealt with unstable housing and unemployment, we called lower class.

The Contemporary Black Marriage Study

The young African-American couples that are the focus of this study share the common experience of being descendants of Africa (and what that means in this world) and of being married in the contemporary

American heterosexual context. Still, they vary in their paths to America, the specifics of their black African heritage, and their assimilation patterns. An in-depth investigation into marital relationships among American-born blacks and black immigrants of various kinds is long overdue. In sum, taking a multiethnic, feminist posture, as *Marriage in Black* does, is critical to revealing the inner-workings of contemporary black marital life. Without such a perspective, many of the nuanced differences among black marriages would be lost. We seek to help expand and contemporize the sociological vision of black marital life and to pinpoint ways in which black marriage can be strengthened through effective, feminist social policy. Here, we make an attempt at balance—a vision of contemporary, heterosexual black marital life that ebbs and flows and that is diverse. It is important to keep in mind that we report on contemporary heterosexual marriages and that we are keenly aware that even in the midst of the madness that was chattel slavery and the madness of other eras that followed, same-sex unions involving African Americans were indeed present and plentiful. This realization has great import given the debate that has raged in the United States over the past two to three decades, but at the time we conducted the interviews, same-sex marriage was not legal nationally or in the area where our couples lived.

We proceed from the progressive perspective on black marriage that suggests that we should move away from talk of black relationship "pathology" in order to offer greater understanding of how social forces come together to produce black marriage that is richly lived. The data used to describe contemporary black marriage was collected from sixty-one mid-Atlantic, American black and white heterosexual couples between 2007 and 2011. The primary method of data collection was intensive interviewing of both husbands and wives, together and individually, but we also employed other methods (see Appendix B). These couples had been married for at least five years. We also interviewed a sample of white couples interviewed for comparative purposes, and the black couples were either spouses who were both born in the United States, or couples in which at least one spouse was black and had been born in an African or Caribbean country. At least one of the spouses was in their thirties (usually both were). Our goal was to gain a deeper and broader understanding of black marital life among younger couples that addresses the importance of class and culture in considerations of black marriage in the United States. We also sought to understand how definitions and experiences of marriage differ among culturally distinct black groups. Twenty of the couples we interviewed are American-born black; in thirteen, one or both spouses immigrated from Africa; in fourteen, one or both spouses immigrated from the Caribbean; and fourteen couples were white (in one of these couples, the husband was a Central Asian immigrant).

Marriage in Black is organized into eight chapters, the first of which you have now read. Because we believe it vital to begin by situating contemporary black marriages within a rich history of events and circumstances, we offer "A Long View of Black Marriage" (Chapter 2) to help ensure that no reader forgets that all black people hail from a rich African and "New World"[56] African-American history—fraught with agony as well as with impressive cultural agency—that influences their current way of life. The empirical chapters that follow begin with "Black Marital Beginnings" (Chapter 3) to provide an understanding of how black couples find each other and decide that marriage is the route they choose to take together. This is followed by "Men and Women, Husbands and Wives: New Perspectives on Egalitarianism" (Chapter 4), a deeper look at how husbands and wives view marital roles and themselves in relation to one another as marital partners. Here, our exploration of contemporary egalitarianism is presented, a subject that has long been of particular interest to us. In Chapter 5, "Contemporary Black Marriage and Parenting," we explore our study couples' beliefs, values, and practices around childbearing and childrearing. Chapter 6, "Is Marriage for Black People?: Ethnic Perceptions of Blacks and the Institution of Marriage," discusses how social institutions, in combinations of intentional and unintentional ways, produce and reinforce ethnic and gender inequalities and the role of certain institutions in shaping black imagery and black marital life. The study couples' perceptions of this is mined largely from their reactions to a newspaper article that prompted Richard Banks' question, "Is marriage for white people?"[57] "Sex, Money, and Beyond: Conflict in Contemporary Black Marriages" (Chapter 7) focuses on the various conflicts in which these families find themselves, conflicts rooted in sex, money, family dynamics, and challenges of daily life. Finally, Chapter 8 ("A New Lens on Black Marriage") offers our reflections on what we have learned, in sum, over the course of this research.

These black couples walked many different paths to marriage. These are their stories.

Notes

1   In this book, "black" and "African American" are used interchangeably to refer to persons of African descent resident in the United States.

2   Raley, R. Kelly, and Larry Bumpass. 2003. "The Topography of the Divorce Plateau: Levels and Trends in Union Stability in the United States after 1980." *Demographic Research* 8:245–260.

3   Cohn, D'Vera, Jeffery S. Passel, Wendy Wang, and Gretchen Livingston. 2011. "Barely Half of U.S. Adults are Married—A Record Low." *Pew Research Center*. Retrieved June 5, 2014 (http://www.pewsocialtrends.org/2011/12/14/barely-half-of-u-s-adults-are-married-a-record-low/).

4   Guzzo, Karen Benjamin. 2009. "Marital Intentions and the Stability of First Cohabitations." *Journal of Family Issues* 30:179–205; Porter, Margaret M., and Arline L. Bronzaf. 1995. "Do the Future Plans of Educated Black Women Include Black Mates?" *The Journal of Negro Education* 64:162–170.

5   To name only a meager few of those contributing recently: Bramlett, Matthew D., and William D. Mosher. 2002. "Cohabitation, Marriage, Divorce, and Remarriage in the United States." *Vital and Health Statistics* 23(22). Hyattsville, MD: National Center for Health Statistics; Orbuch, Terri L., Joseph Veroff, Hamilah Hassan, and Julie Horrocks. 2002. "Who Will Divorce: A 14-year Longitudinal Study of Black Couples and White Couples." *Journal of Social and Personal Relationships* 19:179–202; and Haskins, Ron, and Isabel V. Sawhill. 2016. "The Decline of the American Family: Can Anything Be Done to Stop the Damage?" *The ANNALS of the American Academy of Political and Social Science* 667:8–34.

6   Bachand, Leslie L. and Sandra L. Caron. 2001. "Ties That Bind: A Qualitative Study of Happy Long-Term Marriages." *Contemporary Family Therapy* 23:105–121.

7   McLanahan, Sara, Elisabeth Donahue, and Ron Haskins. 2005. "Introducing the Issue." *The Future of Children* 15:3–12.

8   Amato, Paul R. and Rebecca A. Maynard. 2007. "Decreasing Non-Marital Births and Strengthening Marriage to Reduce Poverty." *Future of Children* 17:117–141; Cowan, Philip A., Carolyn Pape Cowan, and Virginia Knox. 2010. "Marriage and Fatherhood Programs." *The Future of Children* 20:205–230.

9   Blackman, Lorraine, Obie Clayton, Norval Glenn, Linda Malone-Colón, and Alex Roberts. 2005. *The Consequences of Marriage for African Americans: A Comprehensive Literature Review*. New York: Institute for American Values; Cutrona, Carolyn E., Daniel W. Russell, W. Todd Abraham, Janet N. Melby, Chalandra Bryant, and Rand D. Conger. 2003. "Neighborhood Context and Financial Strain as Predictors of Marital Interaction and Marital Quality in African American Couples." *Personal Relationships* 10:389–409.

10   For example, see, Amato et al., 2007; Brown, Susan. 2010. "Marriage and Child Well-Being: Research and Policy Perspectives." *Journal of Marriage and Family* 72:1059–1077; and Christina Gibson-Davis, Kathryn Edin, and Sara McLanahan. 2005. "High Hopes but

Even Higher Expectations: The Retreat from Marriage among Low-income Couples." *Journal of Marriage and Family* 67:1301–1312.

11   Gordon, April. 1998. "The New Diaspora-African Immigration to The United States." *Journal of Third World Studies* 15:79–103; Arthur, John. 2000. *Invisible Sojourners: African Immigrant Diaspora in the United States.* Westport, CT: Praeger Publishers.

12   Roberts, Sam. 2005. "More Africans Enter the U.S. Than in Days of Slavery." *New York Times.* Retrieved June 6, 2014 (http://www.nytimes.com/2005/02/21/nyregion/more-africans-enter-us-than-in-days-of-slavery.html?mcubz=0).

13   Kunkle, Frederick. 2015. "Black Immigration is Remaking the U.S. Black Population, Report Says." *The Washington Post*, April 6. Retrieved September 7, 2017 (https://www.washingtonpost.com/local/black-immigration-is-remaking-us-black-population-report-says/2015/04/09/ded49c58-de29-11e4-a1b8-2ed88bc190d2_story.html?utm_term=.c7e6d595707c).

14   Furdyna, Holly E., M. Belinda Tucker, and Angela D. James, 2008. "Relative Spousal Earnings and Marital Happiness Among African American and White Women." *Journal of Marriage and Family* 70:332–344.

15   Glynn, Sarah J. 2016. "Breadwinning Mothers Are Increasingly the U.S. Norm." *Center for American Progress*, December 19. Retrieved September 7, 2017 (https://www.americanprogress.org/issues/women/reports/2016/12/19/295203/breadwinning-mothers-are-increasingly-the-u-s-norm/).

16   Berk, Sarah Fenstermaker. 1985. *The Gender Factory: The Apportionment of Work in American Households.* New York: Plenum Press.

17   Hochschild, Arlie, and Anne Machung. 2012. *The Second Shift: Working Families and the Revolution at Home.* New York: Penguin Books.

18   Note that Blacks from the Caribbean are often referred to as Afro-Caribbeans.

19   Fogel, Robert W. 2000. *The Fourth Great Awakening and the Future of Egalitarianism.* Chicago: The University of Chicago Press.

20   Kornich, Sabino, Julie Brines, and Katrina Leupp. 2012. "Egalitarianism, Housework, and Sexual Frequency." *Sociological Review* 78:26–50; McDaniel, Anne E. 2008. "Measuring Gender Egalitarianism: The Attitudinal Difference between Men and Women." *International Journal of Sociology* 38:58–80; Schwartz, Pepper. 1995. *Love Between Equals: How Peer Marriage Really Works.* New York: Free Press; Wax, Amy L. 1998. "Bargaining in the Shadow of the Market: Is There a Future for Egalitarian Marriage?" *Virginia Law Review* 84:509–672.

21   King, Lynda, and Daniel King. 1997. "Sex-Role Egalitarian Scale: Development, Psychometric Properties, and Recommendations for Future Research." *Psychoogy of Women Quarterly* 21:71–87.

22   Brighouse, Harry, and Erik Olin Wright. 2008. "Strong Gender Egalitarianism." *Politics & Society* 36:360–372.

23   Gerson, Kathleen. 2010. *The Unfinished Revolution: How a New Generation Is Reshaping Family, Work, and Gender.* New York: Oxford University Press; Wang, Wendy. 2013. "For Younger Adults, the Ideal Marriage Meets Reality." *Pew Research Center.* Retrieved September 4, 2017 (http://www.pewresearch.org/fact-tank/2013/07/10/for-young-adults-the-ideal-marriage-meets-reality); Wang, Wendy, and Paul Taylor. 2011. "Millennials' Attitudes about Marriage." *Pew Research Center.* Retrieved September 4, 2017 (http://www.pewsocialtrends.org/2011/03/09/iii-millennials-attitudes-about-marriage/).

24   Staples, Robert, and Leanor Boulin Johnson. 1993. *Black Families at the Crossroads: Challenges and Prospects.* San Francisco: Jossey-Bass Publishers.

25   Blee, Kathleen M., and Ann R. Tickamyer. 1995. "Racial Differences in Men's Attitudes about Women's Gender Roles." *Journal of Marriage and Family* 57:21–30; Kane, Emily W. 2000. "Racial and Ethnic Variations in Gender-Related Attitudes." *Annual Review of Sociology* 26:419–439.

26 For example, see the work of Beckett, Joyce O., and Audrey Smith. 1981. "Work and Family Roles: Egalitarian Marriage in Black and White Families." *Social Service Review* 55:314–326; Landry, Bart. 1987. *The New Black Middle Class.* Berkeley, CA: University of California Press; Willie, Charles V., and Richard J. Reddick. 2010. *A New Look at Black Families*, 6th ed. Lanham, MD: Rowman & Littlefield Publishers; Roy, Kevin M., and Omari Dyson. "Making Daddies into Fathers: Community-Based Fatherhood." *American Journal of Community Psychology* 45:139–154.

27 Merriam Webster. 2017. "Assimilation." *Merriam-Webster.com.* Retrieved September 4, 2017 (https://www.merriam-webster.com/dictionary/assimilation).

28 Gordon, Milton M. 1964. *Assimilation in American Life: The Role of Race, Religion and National Origins.* New York: Oxford University Press.

29 Shaw-Taylor, Yoku, and Steven A. Tuch, eds. 2007. *The Other African Americans: Contemporary African and Caribbean Families in the United States.* Lanham, MD: Rowman & Littlefield Publishers.

30 Ogbu, John U., and Herbert D. Simons. 1998. "Voluntary and Involuntary Minorities: A Cultural-Ecological Theory of School Performance with Some Implications for Education." *Anthropology and Education Quarterly* 29:155–188.

31 Ogbu, John U. 1978. *Minority Education and Caste: The American System in Cross-Cultural Perspective.* San Diego, CA: Academic Press.

32 Klineberg, Stephen. 2006. "1965 Immigration Law Changed Face of America." WYPR Radio Interview (Baltimore). Retrieved November 10, 2016 (http://www.npr.org/templates/story/story.php?storyId=5391395).

33 Office of the Historian. n.d. "The Immigration and Nationality Act of 1952 (The McCarran–Walter Act)." Bureau of Public Affairs, United States Department of State. Washington, D.C. Retrieved September 4, 2017 (https://history.state.gov/milestones/1945-1952/immigration-act).

34 Until 1967, states had autonomy in determining who could marry, whether this be across racial, religious, or citizenship lines. Some of this state autonomy is described in Washington, R. 2005. "Sealing the Sacred Bonds of Holy Matrimony." *Freedmen's Bureau Marriage Records Genealogy Notes* 37(1). Retrieved January 9, 2018 (https://www.archives.gov/publications/prologue/2005/spring/freedman-marriage-recs.html).

35 Shaw-Taylor and Tuch, 2007.

36 Hao, Lingxin. 2007. *Color Lines, Country Lines: Race, Immigration, and Wealth Stratification in America.* New York: Russell Sage Foundation.

37 Shaw-Taylor and Tuch, 2007.

38 De Augustine Reid, Ira. 1939. *The Negro Immigrant: His Background, Characteristics, and Social Adjustment, 1899–1937.* New York: Columbia University Press.

39 Portes, Alejandro, and Min Zhou. 1993. "The New Second Generation: Segmented Assimilation and Its Variants." *The ANNALS of the American Academy of Political and Social Science* 530:74–96.

40 Ogbu and Simons, 1998.

41 A good discussion of black ethnics and their interracial opinions and attitudes can be found in Greer, Christina M. 2013. "You Win Some, You Lose Some: Hard Work and the Black Pursuit of the American Dream." Pp. 80–112 in *Black Ethnics: Race, Immigration, and the Pursuit of the American Dream.* New York: Oxford University Press.

42 Brown, Victoria. 2015. "In Solidarity: When Caribbean Immigrants Become Black." *NBC News*, March 2. Retrieved May 5, 2015 (http://www.msnbc.com/politicsnation/watch/baltimore-uprising--day-2-436677187644).

43 Smith, Candis W. 2014. *Black Mosaic: The Politics of Black Pan-Ethnic Diversity.* New York: New York University Press.

44 Hao, 2007.

45   Batons, Christie D., Zhenchao Qian, and Daniel T. Litcher. 2006. "Interracial and Intraracial Patterns of Mate Selection Among America's Diverse Black Populations." *Journal of Marriage and Family* 68:658–672.

46   Lincoln, Karen D., Robert Joseph Taylor, and James S. Jackson. "Romantic Relationships among Unmarried African Americans and Caribbean Blacks: Findings from the National Survey of American Life." *Family Relations* 57: 254–266.

47   Kent, Mary Mederios. 2007. "Immigration and America's Black Population." *Population Bulletin* 62(4):3–16.

48   Bernstein, Nina. 2007. "In Secret, Polygamy Follows Africans to N.Y." *New York Times.* Retrieved June 6, 2017 (http://www.nytimes.com/2007/03/23/nyregion/23polygamy. html); Hagerty, Barbara Bradley. 2008. "Some Muslims in U.S. Quietly Engage in Polygamy." *National Public Radio.* Retrieved October 3, 2017 (https://www.npr.org/templates/story/story.php?storyId=90857818).

49   Roopnarine, Jaipaul L. 2013. "Fathers in Caribbean Cultural Communities." Pp. 203–227 in *Fathers in Cultural Context*, edited by David W. Shwalb, Barbara J. Shwalb, and Michael E. Lamb. New York: Routledge.

50   Kempadoo, Kamala. 2009. "Caribbean Sexuality: Mapping the Field." *Caribbean Review of Gender Studies: A Journal of Caribbean Perspectives in Gender and Feminism* 3:1–24.

51   McAdoo, Harriette P., Sinead Younge, and Solomon Getahun. 2007. "Marriage and Family Socialization among Black American and Caribbean and African Immigrants." Pp. 93–116 in *The Other African Americans: Contemporary African and Caribbean Families in the United States*, edited by Yoku Shaw-Taylor and Steven A. Tuch. Lanham, MD: Rowman & Littlefield Publishers.

52   Sudarkasa, Niara. 2007. "Interpreting the African Heritage in African American Family Organization." Pp. 29–47 in *Black Families*, 4th ed., edited by Harriette Pipes McAdoo. Thousand Oaks, CA: Sage Publications.

53   See, for example, Lacy, Karyn. 2007. *Blue-Chip Black Race, Class, and Status in the New Black Middle Class.* Berkley and LA: University of California Press.

54   Oliver, Melvin L., and Thomas M. Shapiro. 2006. *Black Wealth, White Wealth: A New Perspective on Racial Inequality.* New York: Routledge.

55   To understand the range of class definitions, consult the work of Karl Marx, Max Weber, Melvin Kohn, Melvin Oliver and Thomas Shapiro, and Annette Lareau.

56   The "New World" refers to the Western Hemisphere. For our specific purposes, we mean the Americas and the whole of the Caribbean.

57   Banks, Ralph Richard. 2011. *Is Marriage for White People?* New York: Plume.

2

A LONG VIEW OF BLACK MARRIAGE

[Sixo] arranged a meeting with Patsy the Thirty-Mile Woman. It took three months and two thirty-four-mile round trips to do it. To persuade her to walk one-third of the way toward him, to a place he knew ... Sixo painstakingly instructed her how to get there, exactly when to start out, how his welcoming or warning whistles would sound. Since neither could go anywhere on business of their own, and since the Thirty-Mile Woman was already fourteen and scheduled for somebody's arms, the danger was real.

Time never worked the way Sixo thought, so of course he never got it right. Once he plotted down to the minute a thirty-mile trip to see a woman. He left on a Saturday when the moon was in the place he wanted it to be, arrived at her cabin before church on Sunday and had just enough time to say good morning before he had to start back again so he'd make the field call on time Monday morning. He had walked for seventeen hours, sat down for one, turned around and walked seventeen more. Halle and the Pauls spent the whole day covering Sixo's fatigue from Mr. Garner.

—Toni Morison, *Beloved*[1]

Nobel Prize-winner Toni Morrison has been called "Black America's best novelist" in part because she has an uncanny way of tapping into the heart of African and African-American pain and suffering during slavery, and into the ruthlessness of slave masters, lynchers, and other terrorists thereafter. Even as fear of severe punishment was omnipresent during slavery, men and women went to great lengths to form forbidden, intimate bonds with one another. That is, they went to great lengths to marry. Further, friends and kin would often go to great lengths to help bring partners together. Toni Morrison's fictional character, Sixo, was ultimately caught by his slave master when he and his friends attempted to escape the plantation. He called out "Seven-O! Seven-O!" to proudly acknowledge the unborn child in the Thirty-Mile Woman's womb they had created together (29).[2]

Black women love what Sixo represents. They love his passion and his dedication. They long for love like his, but a love that also includes long life and happiness. Black men want the same from women. For such a vision, black men and women today often look back at marriages past, when life in love seemed much more certain and predictable. Sometimes they only need to look back to their own parents' marriages or those of their grandparents. But as sociologist Andrew Billingsley explained in his seminal work, *Climbing Jacob's Ladder: The Enduring Legacy of African-American Families* (1992), the "long view" of history is always the most appropriate.[3]

And so, as we take this far view of history (back to pre-Colonial Africa, slavery in America, Reconstruction, the Great Black Migration), as well as the near past (the welfare state and the modern era), we find that marriage was far more prevalent among blacks "back then" than it is today. And we also know that black marriages have been mired in "blackness," a condition the world has seemed to problematize and indict for its cultural backwardness. The socio-cultural struggle to give black marriage dignity has lasted up until the present day.

Marriage among black people has never been easy. There have been a host of relational, political, economic, and other social factors that have conspired to keep black men and women apart. But in spite of barriers past and present, black marital partnerships of all kinds have continued to be founded and to flourish, even among the couples we met in the new millennium. Because the vast majority of black slaves—transported across the Atlantic to the United States and the Caribbean[4]—hailed primarily from the nations of West Africa, we know that slave marriage (spanning the sixteenth to nineteenth centuries) came from West African cultures. We also have good information on how black marriage evolved through Reconstruction, Jim Crow, the welfare state, the civil rights era, and into the new millennium. This chapter provides an overview of what black marriage looked like across history, how it was transformed over time, and what black marriage looks like in the twenty-first century. The time periods we isolate are not exhaustive, but they do represent major swaths of time when the strength of black people, black families, and particularly black marriages was undermined.[5]

Pre-Colonial Africa

The story of pre-Colonial West Africa is quite dense, as it involves a great number of countries, cities, villages, clans, and cultures that generate a wide range of experiences. It also includes relationships that West Africa had with other areas of Africa and with colonialist powers. Included in this slave history is slavery that existed *within* Africa, a practice that only vaguely resembled the later practice in the Americas. This African version of slavery eventually gave way to trading black slaves for other goods with European colonialists and to forced migration of African slaves out of Africa.[6] Colonists salivated at the thought of large profits from that trade, which led to centuries of forced African enslavement in the United States and the Caribbean. Colonists developed a particular cruelty toward these slaves that ultimately decimated both African and African-American populations.

Marriage and family as they pertain to the transatlantic slave trade are a central subject pursued by anthropologist Niara Sudarkasa. Her essays often begin with details on how marriage in West Africa was practiced before slavery, and then proceed to draw from the long view of history of marriage into the slave era and beyond. From such work, we learn that marriage in historic West Africa was predominantly polygynous, though not exclusively. Polygyny refers in this West African context to a single man being married to multiple wives, where all marital parties and off-spring operate as one family:

> All children of the same generation within the compound regarded themselves as brothers and sisters (rather than some being siblings and others cousins), and since the adults assume some of the same responsibilities toward their nephews and nieces (whom they termed sons and daughters) as they did toward their own offspring, African

conjugal families did not have the rigid boundaries characteristic of nuclear families in the West.[7] (34)

Additionally, the husband–wife partnerships were subsumed *under* the consanguineal core group—persons bound by biology. Married couples were guided by the family core (elders), and ownership of family property was governed by the core. And though multiple couples held strong connections to one another in these families, they each had a good deal of autonomy in decision-making. This form of marriage supported the need for families to have many children who would each contribute to the family's survival, particularly given the intense labor of agrarian society. It also served to create strong bonds among many families. In addition,

> [Polygyny is said to be] socially necessary in order to ensure the continuation of society, and to provide for the needs of the many women who might otherwise never enjoy the status and benefits which accompany being a mother, a bearer of children, and are thus a vital link to the ancestors. Wars between groups often resulted in the reduction of the male population, thus females usually outnumbered males. Unmarried women risked social humiliation without a husband and children, thus the system sought to provide the needs of everyone in the society.[8] (232)

Such details help to refocus attention away from modern-day criticisms of the practice of polygyny and on to how it served positively for African family formation and maintenance, though there is no record of how women felt about it at the time.

Polygynous marriage in pre-Colonial (and Colonial) West Africa also helped create new economic relations with foreign traders and was a strategy to consolidate commercial and political alliances among African families.[9] Interactions with foreigners often led to interracial marriage and mulatto offspring. Such alliances were "endorsed by African political elites" (70–71),[10] and they made for significant female power through slave women's inheriting of property and businesses and their acting as commercial agents. Though frequently sexually exploited, these slave women were often in the position to negotiate freedom for themselves and their offspring.

While some pre-slavery polygynous partnerships became marriages, most operated in concubinage. Such partnerships did not operate under a random set of beliefs and practices. Instead, West African societies, at the village level, developed strong and "elaborate legal codes and court systems that regulated the marital and family behavior of individual members" (1).[11] Marriages focused on the couples, but were also the concern of all members of both families, and marriage was under family and community control. It was the consanguineal core—the biologically linked family—that had the predominant decision-making power. Married couples were brought into the consanguineal residential compound of the husband's family, where property was owned jointly and where spouses did not inherit property from each other. Primacy was given to these blood kin as a means of protecting the family's original joint assets.

Gender relations within marriages of various types have been a major topic within the study of black marriage for some time, perhaps primarily because of the historical practice of polygyny, which on its face appears fiercely patriarchal. But much of this gender discussion has focused on the supposed matriarchal nature of pre-Colonial West African societies, in contrast to the patriarchy by which the rest of the world has operated. This contrast has been made difficult by confusion among terms— matrilineality, matrifocality, and matriarchy.

What most references to matrilineality, pre-Colonial or otherwise, state is that it is a system by which family heritage is traced through the mother and maternal ancestors; that in matrilineal settings, a matriline determines one's inheritance of property and/or title, and works to interlock mothers together across the generations; and that the maternal descent group is central to the functioning of that culture, where in the more modern patrilineal systems, the father's line poses the most meaningful connections made in the family and society at large. However, Liza Debevec, a social anthropologist, cautions us to dig deeper in order to understand that matrilineal systems have not

> necessarily [been] empowering to women ... property is not transferred from one woman to another but rather through a woman's male kin. For example, ownership can be transferred from

the mother's brother to the nephew but by no means to women themselves.[12]

Solien de González (1544)[13] shows us, on the other hand, that matrifocality is "a type of family or household grouping in which the woman is dominant and plays the leading role psychologically." This is a term that appears to have only surfaced around the 1960s[14] and applies particularly to societal contexts where marital stability is not a given (as in the United States, for example); the woman (a mother) provides necessary stability largely through her domestic and workforce contributions. Such a role allows her—some say necessitates her—to exercise authority over others in her domain, particularly in the rearing of children.

Matrifocality and matriarchy are often used interchangeably, even though matrifocality emerges from individual or extended family processes, while matriarchy and matrilineality are both governed at a societal or cultural level. According to Staples and Johnson, "[a] *matriarchy* is formally defined as a system of government ruled by women. This concept implies great advantages for women in the society" (15).[15] While matrilineal and matrifocal patterns are common in various parts of the world, historians and ethnographers have not been successful in seeking out matriarchal societies. According to Tarikhu Farrar, there is no evidence that such societies have ever really existed.[16] What *is* known is that men have consistently wielded the political power and social status in society. Across the globe, men have had authority that gives them power over the lives of women. West Africa is no exception.

But while pre-Colonial West African men held authority in the family and over their wives, women were still highly regarded and were even allowed to control some of their own personal property.[17] Further, the respect of male authority was not taken for granted; to a degree, men had to earn admiration and respect by diligently carrying out their assigned roles. Reverence was then paid by wives to husbands for their attentiveness.[18]

To further clarify the balance of male and female power in this context, Cyrelene Amoah provides this description of domestic gender relations in pre-Colonial Nigerian Yoruba society, for example:

though the Yoruba did not have an ideological conception of two genders, they did distinguish between male and female roles at home. Women's gender-specific responsibilities included cooking meals for the family and child rearing while men were responsible for obtaining the family's farm land and maintaining the compound. Clearly, although it was okay for Yoruba women to earn an income, a woman's domestic duties took precedence. In this regard, male dominance was still present in the daily lives of women, even though their cultural ideology did not define them as a separate category or label them as inferior in physical, emotional, or moral terms.[19] (2)

And Oseni Taiwo Afisi provides further clarification:

In submission therefore, one could say that women have played indispensable roles in traditional Africa. But in spite of the activities, roles, responsibilities and positions women held in traditional Africa, the man in pre-colonial Africa was still the head of the family as well as leader of society; society was purely patriarchal in nature. The man still played the controlling agent in the family; women played supporting roles to the men, and the roles of women were complimentary [sic] to men.[20] (232)

Marital dissolution in these societies often did not have the same kind of stigma that it has currently in Western (and even African) society today. When it was time for a marriage to end, it ended rather simply and with little emotional content. Afterwards, most people remarried, and most men and women lived in marriages for the better part of their lives. The children of these unions remained attached to their natal compounds. Still, marital dissolution was of great significance to the extended families. Marriage was indeed a sacred bond among West Africans, but it was by far not the most important bond in an adult's life. The extended family and those endeared to it had greater significance. And even sexual relations lacked contemporary import: "[I]n the context of polygyny, women as well as men had sexual liaisons with more than one partner."[21] The procreative consequences of this were of no threat to the husband, who was ultimately considered the father of all of his wife's children.

In sum, pre-Colonial West African marriage was quite different from what most Americans have known, particularly in recent decades. And while it is certain that West African slaves carried the memory of their native marriage culture with them in their hearts and minds for some time, they did not have much freedom to practice that which had historically sustained them. New marital arrangements and customs, carrying *some* remnants of the past, emerged in antebellum slavery.

Slavery in America (1526–1865)

Slavery on this side of the Atlantic was universally *chattel* slavery, whereby every slave was purchased to be the personal possession of the slave owner: property. The slave had no rights and was expected to commit 100% of his or her labor (including reproductive labor and sexual favors) to the slave owner. In addition, slaves no longer held their former social statuses, even those of royal background. The 1829 Supreme Court decision (*North Carolina v. Mann*) was potently effective in solidifying slave owners' control over their slaves' lives. Quoting from the state supreme court's judgment on this manner, stated through Judge Thomas Ruffin, Thomas Morris highlights that "'inherent in the relation of master and slave' was the fact that 'the power of the master must be absolute, to render the submission of the slave perfect'" (190).[22] This meant full domination of enslaved Africans, even over their romantic and marital lives.

Chattel status rendered slaves genderless except for their reproductive functions. And while men and women may have been assigned different tasks on the plantation, the work they performed was equally dominating of their personal lives and equally grueling; that is, there was general disregard for gender in the assignment of slave duties.

Perhaps the most vivid images we have of black marriage in slavery reflect the sort of determination we see in *Beloved*'s character Sixo. The intensity of such relationships in this time of peril is reflected in the fact that male slaves often chose to marry women from other plantations because, as John Anderson states, "I did not want to marry a girl belonging to my own place, because I knew I could not bear to see her ill-treated" (129)[23] Still, the risks seemed worth it to many. It has been said that "literally hundreds if not thousands" of male and female slaves were known to have run away in search of their spouse (and other family members as well)[24] when that spouse had been sold away, had run away himself or herself, or was otherwise "lost" from them. Still, by conservative estimates, hundreds of thousands of black slaves went to great lengths to be married in some sense and, therefore, risked having to run away to find their spouse someday and somewhere. In North Carolina alone, many heterosexual slave partners managed to marry during slavery (based on post-slavery records); others were discovered in the District of Columbia and Mississippi.[25]

Morrison's Sixo is one of many enduring figures in American storytelling. The 2013 Academy Award-winning film *12 Years a Slave*, a dramatic adaptation of an 1853 slave narrative memoir, is yet another. *12 Years a Slave* depicted a New York State-born free African-American man, abolitionist Solomon Northup, who was kidnapped away from his family and sold into slavery. Northrup works tirelessly to regain his freedom and return to his wife. The film is yet another fictional account of a black married couple being ripped away from each other at the whim of slave traders, and of the extent to which slaves struggled to be rejoined with significant others. No matter the depth of the love or the fierceness of the commitment, such stories reflect that slaves could not construct marriage on their own terms. Even when a slave master saw an economic advantage in a slave coupling—some masters believed that family life helped to dissuade slaves from running off—he couldn't condone an actual "marriage." Marriage was not legal for slaves. In its place was the "jumping of the broom," a ritual to satisfy the urges of slaves to legally couple. Jumping over the broom represented the couple's commitment to domestic co-existence. Thus, slavery was an era where black men and women had to struggle to maintain a relationship, let alone a marriage, in the midst of tragedy, cruelty, and forced physical separation.[26]

Even the renowned abolitionist and driver of the Underground Railroad, Harriet Tubman, was married during slavery in 1844—to a *free* black man named John Tubman (though their marriage did not ultimately work out).[27] This is a good time to acknowledge that during the time of slavery John Tubman was only one of a substantial population of free blacks in the United States. Andrew Billingsley provides one of many descriptions of free blacks who chose to marry:

Free Blacks followed several patterns of marriage and family life, all heavily influenced by the prevailing conditions and opportunities in the area where they lived. They sometimes married other free Blacks; sometimes they married enslaved Blacks. At other times they married white partners or Native Americans. ... Among the free Blacks who married slaves were Venture Smith and Amos Fortune. Venture Smith, born in Africa, was captured and brought to this country and sold into slavery. In 1765, he was able to purchase his freedom at the age of thirty-six, but his wife and children were still slaves. He worked hard as a woodsman, saved his money, and purchased his wife, his daughter, two sons, and three friends. ... [Amos Fortune] was born in Africa, and as a slave in Massachusetts, he was taught the trades of bookbinding and tannery. In 1770, after serving one master for forty years, he was permitted to purchase his freedom when he was sixty years old. When he was sixty-eight, he purchased a slave woman named Lydia Somerset and married her. She died a few months later in the midst of the Revolutionary War. He then purchased another slave, Violate Baldwin, and married her. They were to have a long and fruitful life together.[28,29]

Thus, as many historians have detailed, black marriage was not something that Africans and their descendants simply copied from whites in America. Their longing to be coupled with one another, as well as with whites and Native Americans, was culturally historic. And it served, in part, to help slaves and beleaguered free blacks survive the most turbulent years of black existence in America.

Reconstruction (1863–1877)

Many African Americans do not recognize July 4, 1776 (Independence Day) or January 1, 1863 (the executive order for the emancipation of slaves) as the mark of their freedom in America. They reserve "Juneteenth" for that—June 19, 1865. Known as "the black people's Fourth of July," this date comes two months after Confederate General Robert E. Lee surrendered and the day that the last community of black slaves were informed by the government that they were actually free. What was to follow Juneteenth was not an era of reparations for the forced labor, lynching, rape, beating, and outrageous aggressions exacted on African Americans, but a time of transforming the Southern states economically to keep them adequately producing goods and services for the nation. And equally, it was a time of regulating black marital lives in order to morally tame African Americans and ensure that they would fall in line with the marital expectations of white America—the very expectations they had been excluded from under slavery.

The Reconstruction Era in the United States is frequently described as a period when the United States established processes to ease newly freed black Americans into citizenship status. But in fact, the government was primarily focused on the economic transformation of the Southern states after the Civil War. That transformation required that black laborers be properly instructed in how to fulfill their economic role as employees and how to live among white people.

Blacks were vital to the labor force during Reconstruction, as they had always been in America; and because the *family* was considered the center of economic activity, the Freedmen's Bureau—charged with implementing a post-Civil War resettlement plan—helped newly freed blacks either to solemnize the intimate relationships they had sustained during slavery or to locate their partners and other loved ones who had been traded and sold across the South. Unofficial spouses were now expected to make their relationships respectable, so much so that the Freedmen's Bureau went practically door to door seeking those who were "cohabiting together as man and wife" and to "take pains to explain to colored persons ... that they [were] firmly married by the operation of the law."[30] It came to light after slavery that close to 50% of the men and 45% of the women had been married for more than five years,[31] so there were many couples to assist in reuniting. Even though marriages under slavery had not been considered legal, they were clearly significant to those blacks who chose to form them.

Without regard for the almost unimaginable cultural shift of slavery to freedom, the Freedmen's Bureau sought to re-create black marriage into the *white* marital form, primarily because blacks had always been defined as "morally and legally unfit to marry" (252)[32] as whites had. The change to a cultural imperative to marry and meet the (white) moral standards of the day meant that black marriage must assume a patriarchal form, with the black husband having superiority over the black wife and the husband being the only spouse who could sign contracts, purchase property, and own the family's resources.[33] Sharecropping was considered the most viable arrangement by which to craft free labor for blacks to trade with others, and it provided for strong Southern economic productivity.

By sharply differentiating the private and public domains of life, work for blacks (as for others) was organized into spheres of "production for subsistence" and "production for exchange" (777),[34] with the latter reserving men as economic and political actors. Under the sharecropping system, work was divided into private and public, the work of the home that kept daily life going, and work that allowed outside earnings and trading goods and services with others. The outside work was generally reserved for men. Under slavery, black men and women had performed the same work, generating income for slave owners. Once black families were expected to adopt relationships that more closely resembled those of whites, women's work lost its equal value; and in freedom, women did not have the same power as men over income and property. Black men, on the other hand, were able to consolidate power over the entire family. They strongly managed the labor of wives and children in the field, sometimes by use of corporal punishment. The black patriarchal family form began taking shape as planned, and Reconstruction made it possible for black men to be recognized as the family head rather than white men solely controlling black wives and families.

Since the nineteenth century, the United States government promoted marriage among blacks to ensure that they did indeed marry and did so properly. Morality and marriage were deeply intertwined, and being moral in matters of sex, childbearing, and general daily living meant getting married. Since blacks were not believed to be civilized in their social interactions, it was believed that the federal government needed to act as the guardian of black marital life and to enforce good marital practices during Reconstruction. Even Southern whites saw it worthwhile to indoctrinate blacks in acceptable marital character and behavior; they believed that this would tame them—especially black men—by reducing their promiscuity, and make it tolerable for whites to live among them.[35] But even Freedmen's Bureau agents were frustrated by the numerous ways in which blacks created marriages that were not like those of whites. Katherine Franke quotes from Freedmen's Bureau documents when she says, "Agents complained that the freed men and women persisted in 'the disgusting practice of living together as man and wife without proper marriage,' and 'living together and calling themselves man and wife as long as it conveniently suits them'" (281).[36]

Therefore, state marriage laws, primarily in the South and named "black codes," were enacted to bring blacks into compliance. The illegality of mixed marriage is the best known of marriage-related black codes, but bigamy laws and laws against fornication and adultery were also erected in reaction to whites' fear of African culture and the context and nature of black relationships. Many blacks were forced to marry persons they would have never considered marrying, and refused to dissolve unofficial marriages they highly valued. The result was a hodgepodge of intimate relationships, many of which were harshly resented, and many of which carried a variety of penalties, such as incarceration and the denial of women's pension benefits.

Though the negativity that surrounded many black intimate lives was also expressed by the Northern black elite (e.g. condemning perceived promiscuity), Franke argues that all blacks "found themselves pulled under by the often-contradictory currents of those who sought to negotiate a number of fundamental social identities and policies through the institution of marriage" (292).[37] By this, she means that as marriages made their way into and through the postbellum period, white marriage was clearly negotiated as a pathway to more production, independence, and agency, whereas black marriage was confined to reproduction and dependency.

In addition to the fear, confusion, and control that surrounded black relationships after the Civil War, African-American relationships had to endure Jim Crow, the system of discrimination and segregation that became the bane of black life (beginning in 1876 and ending in 1965). It was institutionalized primarily in the South, but was a *de facto* phenomenon throughout much of the country. During the Jim Crow reign, any black civil rights gained were in some sense rescinded. Because so much of the controversy rested in the doctrine of segregation, it is no surprise that it was *interracial* intimate relationships and marriages that were particularly targeted during this era. Numerous states passed laws making virtually every form of intimate association between whites and blacks illegal, severely restricting the breadth of what could have been black marital life in its fullest form.

The Transition "Up North" (1910–1970)[38]

> *The migration to the industrial North not only reshaped African-American history but also left its reverberative imprint on Black family life.*
>
> —Donna Franklin[39] (52)

The long period following Reconstruction, referred to as the Great Black Migration, is believed by many scholars to have been the most significant period shaping the lives of African Americans today. While the earlier historical periods (outlined above) certainly made their mark on the life changes of African Americans for generations, the Great Migration (though voluntary) was second only to the Atlantic slave trade in uprooting blacks from their cultural strongholds and unraveling their sense of belonging and security. Sociologist E. Franklin Frazier, in his seminal work first published in 1939,[40] believed (among others) that urban life in the North had corrupted black life and weakened blacks' ability to stave off the many threats against them. Similar ideas were advanced decades later by William Julius Wilson as he observed yet another migratory experience among blacks in the mid-1970s and 1980s: middle-class black migration from the inner-city to the suburbs.[41] Most importantly, the Great Migration would be a mixed blessing for black married couples and their families, and appears to have set the stage for the challenges black families would face for years to come. The move "up north" opened up a new world for a great many African-American couples, but at what cost? Even as they made tremendous strides through the decades in numerous ways, economically, educationally, politically, and otherwise, maintaining strong marital bonds was no easy feat.

The Great Migration came in three waves (approximately 1910–1940, 1941–1965, and 1965 to the present). Pushed by Jim Crow and pulled by the hope of better jobs, education, and housing for themselves and their children, 6 million African Americans left the postbellum South for what they imagined would be peaceful and prosperous Northern and Midwestern cities. This huge proportion of the black population fled the South to settle in areas of the country that promised to be kinder and gentler. According to Clayborne Carson et al.,

> Southern migrants came for economic opportunity, but many also felt they were running for their lives. One New Orleans resident said he came north to escape "the lynchman's noose and the torchman's fire." A black newspaper predicted African American immigrants would "suffer in the North. Some of them will die ... [but] any place would be paradise compared with [the danger in] some sections of the South."[42] (355)

Black ex-slaves from the South left behind poor agricultural conditions in the South and banked on finding more secure jobs with the railroads and factories of various kinds. Their migration proved to be quite diverse in terms of where folks landed; and those blacks who chose to stay put had their own personal set of motivations. As Stewart Tolnay explains,

> In all likelihood, [the Black migrants were] a heterogeneous group, motivated by a plethora of reasons. It is also likely that the characteristics of the migrant population varied over time, as the social and economic forces driving the migration shifted. [43] (212)

Granted, black Southern peasant labor was quite plentiful for white employers to exploit in Northern cities. But there was also an opportunity for blacks to experience freedom in a whole new way: professionally, economically, and socially. The destination cities that are typically highlighted during this time are New York City (Harlem), Philadelphia, Detroit, and Chicago; however, other sources expanded these destinations to places like Los Angeles; Syracuse, NY; Oakland; San Francisco; Denver; Seattle; Milwaukee; Newark, NJ; Gary, IN; New Orleans; Atlanta; Washington, DC; and Baltimore.[44,45]

Free blacks have always lived in America, whether they were free from the start, slaves who received manumission papers along the way, or those granted *mulatto* status. Free blacks tended to live in cities, and they acclimated well to city life and established their own urban "high" culture and social institutions. Further, a good number of newly freed blacks rose to middle-class standing and made their way to the North. But the mixing of established and newer black populations was not smooth and harmonious. Once World War I began, older, more-rooted elite and middle-class Northern black families clashed with the new migrant, Southern ones. These clashes reoccurred for a good while as more and more waves of Southern black migrants moved North, usually in the form of "chain" migration.[46] The migrants were seen by established Northerners as "hordes," "ignorant," "uncouth," and "impoverished" (393).[47] But in time, many of these migrants assimilated to the established black community and even became leaders. This was possible because leaders were in great demand, as Northern industries were desperate to replace white, European immigrant workers who had left when the opportunity to advance in the industrial world came about or when the war called them to duty. But it is not clear whether advances such as these made by Southern black families in entering the North were enough for them to overcome the cultural barriers between them and to form marital unions.

Demographic realities taking shape in the North posed threats to the marital futures of black men and women coming from the South.[48] Black migrants showed social patterns very distinct from whites, with high levels of poverty, joblessness, and related social dislocation, particularly in the city. Life was often difficult for many black men and women struggling to get steady jobs to sustain family life. When they settled in the North, women tended to choose different areas in the city than men did, areas where opportunities for women to make a living were more plentiful. These settlement trends made dating and forming a family difficult at times in some places. The more women that settled in particular areas, the greater the shortage of black men. The gender gap in urban areas where most migrants landed was greatest for young, single blacks. And even when potential marriage partners were relatively plentiful, it was not always easy to meet face-to-face on a regular basis due to difficulty traveling across the city. Further, prospects for marriage were undermined by some of the same problems black men face today: unemployment, imprisonment, and dying young.[49]

For married blacks, migration almost always meant some form of marital separation. Blacks in this era were far more likely to experience family desertion that any other ethnic group.[50] One spouse—often but not always the wife—might stay behind in the South, while the other wrestled with securing regular work with decent wages in the North, sending money home to support the other spouse and children. Such an arrangement put enormous pressure on the working spouse both physically and emotionally, as working hours were long; with vacations nearly unheard of, there was little time for venturing South to visit with family. This made it all too easy for both spouses to find solace in other things and other people during the lonely times. Sometimes, one spouse or the other formed new families. The original family would dissolve, even if divorce was not sought.

Social science scholar Donna L. Franklin, reflecting on E. Franklin Frazier's historical work, finds justification for black men's family desertion in this particular period of migration: It is black men's so-called post-Reconstruction loss of control over family matters. She explains that husbands' desertion of their wives and children was due to "resentment of unstable unemployment and poor working conditions [and to] diminished authority within the family that contributed most to domestic conflicts. ... Some Black men sought to regain some of their autonomy and self-worth by abandoning their families" (79–80).[51] E. Franklin Frazier places the primary blame for all of this marital destabilization on the tremendous challenges of urbanization for black people, namely the long duration of spousal separation.

Then, there was also the draw of Northern life, with its gambling, nightclubs, prostitution, drinking, and drugs. These activities were often more profitable and, to some, more respectable than low-wage factory and other pitiful work in the city. These vices often led to the irresponsible spouse drifting further and further away from the family. Carson also explains that although many migrants chose not to engage in crime to make ends meet, there are plenty of stories about the types of opportunities black Americans grasped in their impatience to make a better life. It also exemplifies the difficulties many black people experienced in transitioning to a cash economy.[52]

Similarly, "stars were born" in the North as well, tearing black marital partners apart, as promises of careers in film, stage, and other arts were scattered all across Northern cities. As is true today, there was always someone lurking about to lure the black man or the black woman into some illicit, lucrative enterprise. Thus, many a black marriage was destroyed by activities in the North that it had almost never been exposed to in the South. Between the physical separation of spouses for weeks, months, and even years at a time, the lure of city vices, and the promises of fast money black marriages were regularly exposed to in the North, it is a wonder any marriage survived at all and that anyone was brave enough to carry on the marriage tradition.

To add insult to injury, black couples struggled through a sharply gendered and fluctuating job market in the North. Franklin's "The Black Male, Industrial Work, and Marital Strains"[53] provides a clear, concise overview of this gendered reality as we entered World War II. While men—black and white—were preoccupied with fighting the war, black women helped to fill the much-needed light-industry jobs in the urban cores (e.g. jobs as cooks, waitresses, maids, ironers, mail order house workers, garment factory workers, food processors, and meat packers). However, as soon as wartime ended and the men were returned to their old positions, black women (and other women) were quickly removed from their posts and were turned back from those well-paying, stable jobs to make way for men. So, as was true before the war, black women were relegated to undesirable, low-wage, unskilled, and semi-skilled positions. And more often than not, black female work was then found in domestic service to white families. In addition, most often black women had to manage the hostility not of men, but of white women who despised having to share spaces with black women—spaces in general, not just work spaces. As a result of this work environment and the sexist ideas about a black woman's worth, black women realized fewer economic gains than black men in these times.[54] Black spouses found themselves competing against each other in the job market.

Over time, the black population of major Northern cities continued to grow by large percentages, and jobs could be found in places like factories, slaughterhouses, and foundries, though the work required was strenuous and sometimes dangerous. But here again, gender differences were stark: women migrants in these times found this work much harder to come by than did men. Still, women could always fall back on domestic-service work. In fact, by the end of World War II, the proportion of black women in domestic service had grown quite a bit. All that black women had managed to prove about their industrial capabilities was moot. Now back to meager wages and irregularly scheduled hours, and often having been deserted by their spouses, they resorted to all that was left to support them: the welfare system.

Black men could not rely on the regularity of work to come along and provide the dignity of a regular family contribution. While organizational efforts helped to make way for approximately 100,000 black men to be enlisted in non-combat units of the army during World War II, the paychecks gained turned out not to be worth the cost of lives lost and discrimination waged again them by their own forces. It was said that black men traded the "mind-numbing sameness of picking cotton" in the South for the North's "mind-numbing sameness of turning a leveler or twisting a widget or stoking a flame for a tiny piece of a much larger thing he had no control over" (316).[55] Whether it was this or the Army, they worked for virtually no wages at all. It was often explained to black men that as much as businesses and unions needed and wanted them to work for them, they knew that the white workers would revolt. There had been numerous reports of problems with white employee morale, walkouts, and resentment when blacks were brought in. Ultimately, black men "found themselves at the bottom looking up" (318)[56] at all of the immigrants, whites, and more-favored blacks from the North towering over them in desperately needed jobs. The result was a severe and regular blow to the black man's ego in the midst of so many black migrant-related strains, making forming and maintaining marital unions that much more challenging.

So, black marriage faced economic struggles that were not only about the lack of wages brought into the home, but about blacks' cultural principles, which were contrary to American cultural principals. Black *women* were more often the spouse best able to earn a family wage. Despite the greater difficulty, black women made a respectable financial contribution fairly consistently above or at least alongside their husbands. However, in acquiring the meager wages necessary to feed, clothe, and house their families, they were forced to endure indignities such as strong tongue-lashings by "highbrow" white wives; being picked through in public like a barrel of tomatoes hoping to be seen as the most appropriate black woman to grace a certain white family's home; and the cruelty of being worked to the bone from sunup to sundown without seeing one's family.

For both black husbands and wives, the North put new and more painful demands on black marriage. In addition to the challenges already discussed, socio-environmental factors such as depressed fertility, the increase in out-of-wedlock births, and new forms of sexual relations created additional strain. Not that marriage had not been challenging in the South, but now marriage had to constantly adjust to the new world in which black couples were interacting. This new environment held promise for the black middle class and elite, but many black couples toiled in the midst of deep racism and complex poverty. The issues arising from this Great Migration—including the challenges of learning to live among not only Northern whites but among free blacks across class and culture—confront black marital lives to this very day. In its most contemporary iteration, these issues also include the complexity of inter-racial, interreligious, and interethnic marriage.

Black Marriage, Social Policy, and the Welfare State

The social welfare of captured African people was never a priority for Americans, except to ensure that their market value and productivity as slaves were preserved. The agenda in the era of legal slavery was to contain, pacify, and demoralize black people. Granted, eventually Northern abolitionists boldly fought for blacks' humanity and vigorously sought to protect them from harm; but neither the Civil War, the Emancipation Proclamation, nor other grand gestures ever placed blacks' welfare over—or even equal to—the interests of whites.

Reconstruction and its Freedmen's Bureau (discussed above), the first attempt at creating social policy to help African Americans, attempted a road toward equality. But that attempt ultimately led to blacks facing nearly the same humiliation and deprivation as they had in slavery. Further, when Reconstruction could have been a set of policies allowing for African Americans to fashion community and home life in their own way, including African customs, it instead emphasized crafting black marriages that mirrored white marriages, including the requisite patriarchal rules (without social or financial support to realistically enact them). Reconstruction, then, could be considered the first act of social policy for blacks and black marriage, but one that ultimately undermined black marital life rather than supported its advancement.

The federal government's general promotion of marriage among black people began even before Reconstruction and could be considered one of the earliest attempts at social welfare policy toward blacks. Constructing welfare policy was believed to be necessary given the savage and uncivilized nature of the African people. General Ulysses S. Grant commissioned the first "contraband camp" in Tennessee, where blacks could camp while they "began to establish themselves as free persons … attending schools established by benevolent organizations … holding political rallies and emancipation celebrations, marrying legally for the first time, and establishing churches."[57] Under slavery, men and women were commonly forced into sexual relations to create more slaves, and women were frequently raped by masters or other powerful whites. By contrast, in contraband camps Christian marriage was the only acceptable sexual relationship between men and women. Outside of Christian marriage, blacks could face prosecution for such things as fornication and adultery, or for being adulterers and bigamists.[58]

During the Jim Crow era, segregation was to be upheld at all costs, and as there was a frenzied obsession with whites—especially white women—not having any sexual contact with blacks, a third set of social policies emerged. These were primarily "anti-miscegenation laws," prohibiting interracial marriage. Black and white men and women found guilty of miscegenation were formally threatened with fines and jail time, even within the less aggressive District of Columbia law:

> If any white man or woman shall intermarry with a negro or mulatto bond or free, such a white man or woman, and such a negro or

mulatto, shall upon conviction or indictment pay a fine of thirty dollars and suffer six months confinement at hard labour. [59] (219)

Laws were also reinforced unofficially through vigilante violence—primarily the lynching of black men when whites perceived that they had expressed any sexual interest in white women. State anti-miscegenation laws were allowed to remain in place until 1967, when *Loving v. Virginia* declared them unconstitutional as a violation of the Fourteenth Amendment's Equal Protection Clause.

Perhaps the most well-known social policy debate regarding African-American marriage and families was embodied in a government document written in 1965 by then-presidential aide and future United States senator Daniel Patrick Moynihan (1927–2003), a document commonly called "The Moynihan Report."[60] The "Negro problem" in the nation was whittled down to one fundamental issue: the instability of its unskilled, poorly educated, urban families. It is worth stating that many scholars believe this document to have been grossly over-quoted and even grossly misinterpreted; but still, after more than fifty years, it is frequently referenced. Far too often, the Moynihan Report is read as a study of the instability of *all* black families and still seen as relevant or even prophetic.[61] While the problems the report brings out are not unique to the lower classes, they are far more prevalent within these lower-class groups, and these are the problems that quickly overtook the conversation.

Each of the issues signifying black family instability in the Moynihan Report implicates black marriage. These issues are: high rates of ever-married women who are subsequently divorced, separated, or living apart from their husbands; a high out-of-wedlock childbearing rate; a large proportion of families headed by women;[62] and a large and increasing welfare dependency (ADC/AFDC) rate, suggesting a lack of a father's income. The Report consulted a number of social science experts to get at the root of why these issues are more prevalent and more problematic among blacks than whites. It asserted that slavery was such a profoundly violent and debilitating experience that its effects have had deep, lasting effects:

Negroes in bondage, stripped of the African heritage, were placed in a completely dependent role. All of their rewards came, not

from individual initiative and enterprise, but from absolute obedience—a situation that severely depresses the need for achievement
among all peoples. Most important of all, slavery vitiated family
life. ... Since many slave owners neither fostered Christian marriage among their slave couples nor hesitated to separate them on
the auction block, the slave household often developed a fatherless
matrifocal (mother-centered) pattern.

It also found that the Reconstruction and Jim Crow eras subjected African
Americans to a host of hazards, severe marginalization and dependency,
and persecuted them hostilely. Perhaps most importantly, it singles out
the black male as having stood no chance of practicing a strong role
given adversities that humiliated him and stunted his growth as a man
and provider. On the other hand, the female was forced to persevere and
take charge of family and married life. This is why she continued to com-
mand the power she did, however inappropriate (according to the beliefs
of the report's authors) that might be.

Other sections of the report follow in much the same way, focusing
on the trials of Northern urbanization in the black family, the unemployment and poverty that awaited there, the unique difficulty black men had
in gaining an economic foothold in the city, and the struggles of black
family life that ensued (though nothing about black women's employment difficulties). It further states:

> There would seem to be an American tradition, agrarian in its
> origins but reinforced by attitudes of urban immigrant groups, to
> the effect that family morality and stability decline as income and
> social position rise. Over the years, this may have provided some
> consolation to the poor, but there is little evidence that it is true.
> On the contrary, higher family incomes are unmistakably associated
> with greater family stability—which comes first may be a mat-
> ter of conjecture, but the conjunction of the two characteristics
> is unmistakable.

Lastly, the report finds the American wage system insensitive to the needs
of individual families, particularly those with an absent father, or simply
those whose incomes are too low to meet their basic needs (incomes

reduced by the rapid increase in black population size). Again, the gender dynamic is raised:

> Because in general terms Negro families have the largest number of children and the lowest incomes, many Negro fathers cannot support their families. Because the father is either not present, is unemployed, or makes such a low wage, the Negro woman goes to work. ... This dependence on the mother's income undermines the position of the father and deprives the children of the kind of attention, particularly in school matters, which is now a standard feature of middle-class upbringing.

Perhaps the most stinging pronouncements of this report are those that seem to place the problems of the black family (and the black community at large) on the backs of black women by speaking of the black matriarchy, a reversal of the "natural order" of marital authority and dominance. It was only a small part of this controversy, but it subsequently brought the ire of many black feminists and sociologists who believed the report was sidetracking the real, central issue: that the elements of black family life that smacked of backwardness were the result of historical forces, racism, and poverty, not black cultural construction.

The numerous voices raised in support or dissent of the Moynihan Report's claims are too many and veer too far away from the purpose of this text. Suffice it to say that every issue raised in 1965 is still being raised today, along with many more. And no social policy direction was given in this report (as was its intention); indeed, over the decades of attention to black marital dilemmas, few specific remedies have been suggested or implemented for bolstering the social welfare of black married couples.

The Modern Era of Black Marriage: Into the Twenty-First Century

The Moynihan Report coincided with many social changes that accelerated in the 1960s. The Civil Rights Act of 1964 made it illegal to discriminate—based on race or sex—when making decisions about hiring, promotions, or employment termination.[63] The Civil Rights Act was followed by the Immigration and Nationality Act of 1965, which allowed increased immigration from Africa and the Caribbean, and the Voting Rights Act of 1965, which removed state barriers designed to prevent black Americans from voting. These race-based reforms were further followed by anti-poverty programs spurred by President Lyndon Johnson's War on Poverty, court decisions that gave legal rights to children born outside of marriage, and legalization of no-fault divorce. The American social landscape was changing quickly for black families, poor families, immigrant families, and families in general.

Today, many scholars cheer the progressive nature of these initiatives, arguing they did much to alleviate poverty and increase social equality. But others argue that social progress has hurt families, and perhaps black families in particular. While some scholars have pointed out that most mothers did not remain on welfare for long periods and that welfare programs designed to assist mothers did not offer enough to make ends meet,[64] others cited government assistance as the root of family breakdown. In *Losing Ground*,[65] Charles Murray argues that welfare programs were not just ineffective, but harmful. Among other ills, Murray believed welfare payments were set up in a way that encouraged women to have children outside of marriage, offering a financial incentive that replaced the need for a husband and father in the house.

Murray's arguments helped to spearhead the federal Personal Responsibility and Work Opportunity Reconciliation Act of 1996, commonly referred to as "welfare reform." Enacted under the Clinton administration, the program radically changed welfare policy, limiting the number of years that poor mothers could receive cash assistance, implementing work requirements, and creating programs to encourage marriage. Despite these reforms, marriage rates continued to decrease, childbearing outside of marriage continued to increase, and a new wave of poverty was created so deep that by 2011, 1.5 million American households with children lived on cash income of less than $2 per day per family member.[66] The number of such households has more than doubled since implementation of 1996 welfare reform. Still, some scholars and political pundits, such as Kay Hymowitz,[67] argue that black families were better off before the reforms of the 1960s because, despite more widespread poverty, children were more likely to grow up in two-parent families.

Others have pointed out different ways public assistance affects lower-income couples who would like to marry. While, on average, marriage leads to higher incomes and reduces child poverty, for those on the lower end of the income scale, marriage can actually make couples less financially stable.[68] Legally creating a single "household income" through marriage can mean couples lose government support that each parent might have been eligible for if they had remained single, including childcare subsidies, Medicaid, Temporary Assistance for Needy Families (TANF), the State Children's Health Insurance Program (SCHIP), the Special Supplemental Nutrition Program for Women, Infants, and Children (WIC), the Earned Income Tax Credit (EITC), Supplemental Nutrition Assistance Program (SNAP), and more.[69] Policy analysts such as Murray and Hymowitz might argue that reducing such programs would force couples to marry, but another approach could be to expand these programs so that marrying did not create a penalty on needed benefits.

It is true that marriage rates have decreased dramatically since the 1960s. The average age of first marriage has increased, divorce rates have increased (though they leveled off after the 1980s), childbearing outside of marriage has increased, and cohabitation is close to universal among young adults (and many in cohabitating relationships do marry eventually). But these changes have occurred for all Americans—not just black Americans or poor Americans. Though marriage is more common among the middle and upper classes and the more educated (true for black Americans as well as those of other races), marriage still occurs among the poor. Black Americans are more likely than whites or Hispanics to say that it's very important to get married if a couple plans to spend their lives together.[70] Despite history, despite social change, despite institutional barriers, black couples still want to marry.

Notes

1   Morrison, Toni. 2004. *Beloved*. New York: Vintage Books.
2   Morrison, 2004.
3   Billingsley, Andrew. 1992. *Climbing Jacob's Ladder: The Enduring Legacy of African-American Families*. New York: Simon & Schuster.
4   The first slaves arrived in Hispaniola (now Haiti and the Dominican Republic) to support the economy of the New World in 1502. Cuba would receive its first slaves in 1513, Jamaica in 1518. Slaves were later exported to Honduras and Guatemala in 1526,

the same year that slaves were brought to North America as part of a Spanish attempt to colonize South Carolina near Jamestown. (See "Atlantic Slave Trade," Wikipedia.com.)

5 We speak in broad generalities when it comes to the vast continent of Africa and the Caribbean, though we are cognizant that the variations in country experience have been quite pronounced in these regions. Nonetheless, we believe the lessons to be learned can still be understood from the broad strokes and applied to those Africans living in the United States.

6 Ojo, Olatunji, and Nadine Hunt, eds. 2012. *Slavery in Africa and the Caribbean: A History of Enslavement and Identity Since the 18th Century*. New York: I. B. Tauris Publishers.

7 Sudarkasa, Niara. 2007. "Interpreting the African Heritage in African American Family Organization." Pp. 29–47 in *Black Families*, 4th ed., edited by Harriette Pipes McAdoo. Thousand Oaks, CA: Sage Publications.

8 Afisi, Oseni Taiwo. 2010. "Power and Womanhood in Africa: An Introductory Evaluation." *The Journal of Pan African Studies* 3:229–238, as cited in Dobson, Barbara. 1954. "Polygamy and Women's Place in Africa." *Corona: Journal of African Cultural Studies* 1: 454–457

9 Candido, Mariana P. 2012. "Concubinage and Slavery in Beneguela, c. 1750–1850." Pp. 65–84 in *Slavery in Africa and the Caribbean: A History of Enslavement and Identity Since the Eighteenth Century*, edited by Olatunji and Nadine Hunt. New York: I. B. Tauris Publishers.

10 Candido, 2012.

11 Staples, Robert, and Leanor Boulin Johnson. 1993. *Black Families at the Crossroads: Challenges and Prospects*. San Francisco: Jossey–Bass Publishers.

12 Debevec, Liza. 2015. "Setting the Record Straight: Matrilineal Does Not Equal Matriarchal." CGIAR Research Program on Water, Land and Ecosystems. Retrieved September 9, 2017 (https://wle.cgiar.org/people/liza-debevec).

13 Solien de González, Nancie L. 1965. "The Consanguineal Household and Matrifocality." *American Anthropologist* 67(December): 1541–1549.

14 Solien de González (1965) states, somewhat surprisingly, that she has been credited with having conceptualized the matrifocal family in her 1959 publication *The Consanguineal Household among the Black Carib of Central America*. Ann Arbor: University of Michigan (dissertation).

15 Staples and Johnson, 1993.

16 Farrar, Tarikhu. 1997. "The Queenmother, Matriarchy, and the Question of Female Political Authority in Precolonial West African Monarchy." *Journal of Black Studies* 27: 579–597.

17 Sudarkasa, 2007.

18 Staples and Johnson, 1993.

19 Amoah, Cyrelene. 2009. "Women in Precolonial and Colonial Yorubaland." Review of McIntosh, Marjorie Keniston, *Yoruba Women, Work, and Social Change. H-Net Reviews* (April). Retrieved September 9, 2017 (http://www.h-net.org/reviews/showrev.php?id=24499).

20 Afisi, 2010.

21 McAdoo, Harriette Pipes (ed.) 2007. *Black Families*. Thousand Oaks, CA: Sage Publications.

22 Morris, Thomas D. 1996. *Southern Slavery and the Law, 1619–1860*. Chapel Hill, NC: University of North Carolina Press.

23 Anderson, John. 1863. *The Story of the Life of John Anderson: the Fugitive Slave*. Edited by Harper Twelvetrees. London: William Treedee, 337, Strand, W.C.

24 A fugitive slave could face brutal punishment if caught, including suffering the amputation of limbs, beatings, or worse. And those aiding and abetting fugitive slaves faced harsh penalties as well.

25 See Billingsley, 1992; and Franklin, Donna L. 1997. *Ensuring Inequality: The Structural Transformation of the African American Family*. New York: Oxford University Press.

26 Parry, Tyler D. 2015. "Married in Slavery Time: Jumping the Broom in Atlantic Perspective." *The Journal of Southern History* 81: 273–312.

27   See "Harriet Tubman." *Biography.com*. Retrieved January 13, 2018 (https://www.biography.com/people/harriet-tubman-9511430). Also find general information about free blacks at "Free Blacks in the Antebellum Period: Part 1." *African American Odyssey*. Retrieved January 12, 2017 (http://lcweb2.loc.gov/ammem/aaohtml/exhibit/aopart2.html) and at Free Negro." *Wikipedia.com*. Retrieved January 13, 2018 (https://en.wikipedia.org/wiki/Free_negro).

28   Excerpts from Billingsley, 1992, pp. 98–101.

29   It is also important to note, however, that many free blacks, pre- and post-Emancipation, chose to form intimate relationships but *not* marry.

30   Washington, Reginald. 2005. "Sealing the Sacred Bonds of Holy Matrimony." *Freedmen's Bureau Marriage Records*, 37(1). Also see Carson, Clayborne, Emma J. Lapsansky, and Gary B. Nash. 2011. *The Struggle for Freedom: A History of African Americans*. Combined Volume, 2nd ed. London: Pearson.

31   Billingsley, 1992.

32   Franke, Katherine M. 1999. "Becoming a Citizen: Reconstruction Era Regulation of African American Marriages." *Yale Journal of Law & the Humanities* 11:251–309.

33   Franklin, Donna L. 1997. "Sharecropping and the Rural Proletariat." Pp. 19–35 in *Ensuring Inequality: The Structural Transformation of the African American Family*. New York: Oxford University Press.

34   Mann, Susan A. 1989. "Slavery, Sharecropping, and Sexual Inequality." *Signs: Journal of Women in Culture & Society* 14:774–798.

35   Pilgrim, David. 2012. "The Brute Caricature." *Jim Crow Museum of Racist Memorabilia*. Retrieved September 9, 2017 (https://ferris.edu/jimcrow/brute/).

36   Franke, 1999.

37   Franke, 1999.

38   "Up north" actually also encapsulates black migration to points Northeast, Midwest, and West during "The Great Migration" of American blacks from the South after Emancipation. The period is marked differently depending on the author's intent. Most references state that this period ran from 1910 to 1970. Others isolate 1915–1960 as the "initial" phase of this migration, where "the majority of migrants moved to major northern cities such as Chicago, Illinois, Detroit, Michigan, Pittsburgh, Pennsylvania, and New York, New York." There was a waning of migration during the World War II era, but migration did continue through the 1970s when blacks settled more and more to the west, to places like Los Angeles, Oakland, San Francisco, Portland, and Seattle. More recently, many blacks have begun migrating back to the South. See BlackPast.org. 2017. "The Great Migration (1915–1960) (http://www.blackpast.org/aah/great-migration-1915-1960); and Stack, Carol. 1996. *A Call to Home: African Americans Reclaim the Rural South*. New York: Basic Books.

39   Franklin, 1997.

40   Frazier, E. Franklin. 1939. *The Negro Family in the United States*. Chicago: University of Chicago Press.

41   Wilson, William J. 1987. *The Truly Disadvantaged: The Inner City, the Underclass, and Public Policy*. Chicago: University of Chicago Press.

42   Carson et al., 2011.

43   Tolnay, Stewart E. 2003. "The African American 'Great Migration' and Beyond." *Annual Review of Sociology* 29:209–232.

44   See Wilkerson, Isabel. 2010. *The Warmth of Other Suns: The Epic Story of America's Great Migration*. New York: Vintage Books; and Carson et al., 2011.

45   See Table 14.1 in Carson et al., 2011, p. 356.

46   "Chain migration" is where immigrants and their relatives follow each other over time to a new country.

47   Frazier, 1939.

48 White, Katherine J. Curtis, Crowder, Kyle, Tolnay, Stewart E., and Robert M. Adelman. 2005. "Race, Gender, and Marriage: Destination Selection During the Great Migration." *Demography* (42):215–241.

49 White et al., 2005.

50 Franklin, 1997.

51 Franklin, 1997.

52 Carson et al., 2011.

53 Franklin, 1997.

54 Trotter, Joe William, Jr. 1991. *The Great Migration in Historical Perspective: New Dimensions of Race, Class, and Gender.* Bloomington, IN: Indiana University Press.

55 Wilkerson, 2010.

56 Wilkerson, 2010.

57 Lovett, Bobby L. 2010. "Contraband Camps." *The Tennessee Encyclopedia of History and Culture.* Retrieved September 9, 2017 (http://tennesseeencyclopedia.net/index.php).

58 Franke, 1999.

59 Monahan, Thomas. 1977. "Interracial Marriage in a Southern Area: Maryland, Virginia, and the District of Columbia." *Journal of Comparative Family Studies,* 8(2):217–241.

60 United States Department of Labor, Office of Policy Planning and Research. 1965. *The Negro Family: The Case for National Action.* Retrieved March 3, 2006 (http://www/dol/gov/oasam/programs/history/webid-moynihan.htm).

61 Italicized here to emphasize this language that is often missed or misrepresented. Too often, the report is believed to reflect all black families.

62 The term "headed" in this context has been nebulously applied for decades.

63 The U.S. National Archives and Records Administration. 2017. "The Civil Rights Act of 1964 and the Equal Employment Opportunity Commission." Retrieved August 15, 2017 (https://www.archives.gov/education/lessons/civil-rights-act/).

64 Edin, Kathryn, and Laura Lein. 1997. *Making Ends Meet: How Single Mothers Survive Welfare and Low-Wage Work.* New York: Russell Sage Foundation.

65 Murray, Charles. 1984. *Losing Ground: American Social Policy, 1950–1980.* New York: Basic Books.

66 Edin, Kathryn and H. Luke Shaefer. 2016. *$2.00 a Day: Living on Almost Nothing in America.* New York: Mariner Books.

67 See Hymowitz's biography at https://www.manhattan-institute.org/expert/kay-s-hymowitz/.

68 Thomas, Adam, and Isabel Sawhill. 2005. "For Love and Money? The Impact of Family Structure on Family Income." *The Future of Children* 15:57–74.

69 Carasso, Adam, and C. Eugene Steuerle. 2005. "The Hefty Penalty on Marriage Facing Many Households with Children." *The Future of Children* 15:151–175.

70 Wang, Wendy, and Kim Parker. 2014. "Record Share of Americans Have Never Married: As Values, Economics and Gender Patterns Change." *Pew Research Center.* Retrieved May 21, 2014 (http://www.pewsocialtrends.org/2014/09/24/chapter-1-public-views-on-marriage/).

3

BLACK MARITAL BEGINNINGS

Suddenly he (Paul D) remembers Sixo trying to describe what he felt about the Thirty-Mile Woman. "She is a friend of my mind. She gather me, man. The pieces I am, she gather them and give them back to me in all the right order. It's good, you know, when you got a woman who is a friend of your mind."

—Toni Morrison, *Beloved*

Rahim Yabu is from Sierra Leone, and his wife, Joyce, is African-American. They met through her mother, who would often have conversations with Rahim while on their jobs cleaning offices. Rahim said, "Most of the time when I go down there, I'm a friendly person—we became friends, we started talking, talking, talking. She told me that she has a daughter, she's gonna introduce me to her daughter. Then she introduced us. So, we talked over the phone ... we went on a date. We went to the movie. So, we started talking, talking for a while, then she got pregnant. She's pregnant for me, and it's my first baby, and I'm going to engage her. I did it. So the time when the baby was born, I looked at the baby and thought, it's my baby! Married her. Went to the courthouse. Do what you gotta do. It's not the outside part of Joyce I like, it's the inside."

In 1865, with the passage of the Thirteenth Amendment to the Constitution, previously enslaved blacks were finally afforded the right to legally marry—though, as we know, this did not extend to same-sex or interracial marriages.[1] From the time of their capture in Africa and throughout their enslavement in the West, blacks in the United States faced tremendous barriers to entering into marriages that were accepted as legal. Most other groups of people around the world did not experience this problem, including Africans living in Africa prior to the slave trade. It took until 1967 for blacks in the United States to win the right to marry people of any race.[2] And then finally, in 2015, a landmark Supreme Court decision established a national right to same-sex marriage, overturning the Defense of Marriage Act (DOMA). This gave couples of all races the right to marry within their sex and legitimized the kinds of same-sex relationships that had existed throughout history. Because all the interviews described herein occurred before the overturning of DOMA, they were conducted only with *heterosexual* married couples. The primary objective of this chapter is to reveal the diverse transitions within contemporary black marriage, and to introduce the reader to many of the black couples whose stories are laced throughout subsequent chapters.

The desire of black men and women to form marital unions has been very strong throughout American history. We observe this same desire in the stories told to us by contemporary black couples, even as statistical research consistently reports significantly less marriage and more divorce among blacks as compared to other racial/ethnic groups. Blacks' desire to marry strongly persists despite all of the issues that plague the black population. But because research on marriage among blacks has been sorely lacking, little is known about the everyday inner workings of their marriages. This is undoubtedly due to the inordinate research focus on black divorce and non-marriage. We sought to better understand these inner workings by focusing on a young cohort of black couples set in contemporary context.

Historically, people of color have been evaluated on their marital activities vis-à-vis whites. White marriages—particularly among the middle class—have been considered to be the *norm*. A host of statistics suggests that black marriages involve relationship dynamics that can differ greatly from those of whites. However, we know very little about what variation may exist among black ethnics. We began this analysis for

Marriage in Black by focusing on the study couples' marital beginnings. We analyzed our interview discussions of marriage formation to determine whether the couples' experiences were patterned in any way by ethnicity and/or social class. In doing so, we were careful to not buy into the notion that whites inherently form romantic relationships that are more robust than others'.

Transforming marital desire into action always involves an initial meeting, dating, and/or courtship,[3] and a legal ceremony of some kind. The study couples' relationship trajectories took on a number of forms, with differing levels of happiness and/or difficulty. In what follows, we provide some understanding of the similarities and differences that exist among the ethnicities and social class groups represented.

The spouses of these study couples are by research design generally of the same ethnic background. However, based on black population research, such as that reported by Mary Maderios Kent in 2007,[4] we were not altogether surprised to find some exceptions. Kent reports that there were more than a million American-born black children who were either immigrants themselves or that had one parent who was foreign born (12). Thus, it is not unusual that a Caribbean or African couple (by our definition) has one spouse that is American-born. Eight of the Caribbean study couples and five of the African couples have a spouse who is American-born. Further, four of the white couples include an Uzbekistani immigrant, a Puerto Rican immigrant, or an African. Among the couples we label as American-born, both spouses are American-born blacks, with the single twist where one wife of an American-born black is biracial (white mother, black father).

As for social class, we found some variation within each ethnic group of study couples (see Appendix A). Across the ethnic groups, our white couples spanned a similar social-class range as our black couples. The American-born black couples tend to be more from the working class. The African couples are equally likely to be working class and middle class. The Caribbean couples tend to be from the middle class. The nature of our sampling procedure did not yield any couples from the upper middle class or the upper classes. Our future work will involve a more intentional approach to include such couples.

Finding Each Other[5]

The initiation of a romantic relationship has changed dramatically over the past twenty years or so. For example, it has been some time since the parents of a young couple were the primary players in bringing the couple together (this was primarily true among white Americans, though it is now still true among some immigrant groups). And with the technological age came the advent of Internet dating, where people use online matchmaking software to help identify highly compatible and attractive partners. Two chapters in Coleman and Ganong's book speak very optimistically about the ability of the Internet to facilitate the initiation and maintenance of romantic relationships.[6] A study published in the *Journal of Proceedings of the National Academy of Sciences*[7] reports that of those married between 2005 and 2012, more than 1 in 3 had met their spouse online. Note, however, that only one of the sixty-one couples interviewed for this research met on the Internet—Ethan and Candy Springfield, a white working-class couple.

Our study couples shared a number of common elements when it came to their marital beginnings. We first considered employing the theoretical notion of "assortative mating"[8] as a starting point for this analysis. Assortative mating (from the sociological perspective) refers to a pattern of romantic relationship-building based on social categories: race, religion, socioeconomic status, age, educational status, and broad attitudinal and demographic *similarities*. Sociologists more often refer to this as "social homogamy," meaning social same-ness. The assumption is that men and women rarely go beyond their *own kind* when it comes to selecting a mate. However, we decided to take a more inductive stance and take at face value the reasons our study couples gave for why they entered into the marital unions they did, and then explore what appeared to be assortative in nature. That is, we remained committed to allowing the empirical data to tell the stories, stories which we found to reflect in good part whether the couples had met in the United States, the Caribbean, or in Africa.

Most American-born black study couples met through a friend or relative, or at school or work. Marlon Byrd's friend reported to him early on that Gwen "was fine" and "had a fat butt." To Marlon, that was a great start. Joking aside, Marlon also liked that Gwen was "a homebody, was down to earth, was no-nonsense." He also liked that she was opinionated and could "stand up to me." Gwen was persuaded to grow closer to him when he professed, "Come on! I'm not like the other guys—dadada this, dadada that. All right, just to prove you wrong, we gonna start dating!"

Quin and Carla Long met while playing basketball at a local state university ("she *tried* to guard me"), and they continued playing together throughout their eight years of dating. He was a college sophomore and she was a freshman. They lovingly joked about how the two of them have never agreed on the details of how they met: "She likes to change the story up a lot!" As Carla described the early days with Quin, she recalled that he "was a nice person, a good person, a friend. He grew on me."

On the whole, the meeting of African-American mates was described in terms like "kismet," and these couples were much more expressive than the other study couples about what attracted them to each other. For example, terms of endearment such as "baby," my "trophy," my "perfect woman," and "my queen" are prominent among the men. The women, while also vocal about their physical attraction to the men, were more likely to be impressed by a man being "decent," by his being someone who behaved or treated them like they were special (a "gentleman"), and by his showing interest in children (whether the woman's own children or not). Charlene Kelly spoke of her mate as "a one-woman man who takes more than just your looks to turn his head," something she found quite comforting.

There were two experiences that were more distinctive among these American-born black couples. One experience was that of meeting their mates when they were very young, as young as middle school-aged. This means that by the time we encountered them, some had been together for twenty years or more. Kristina Erickson said that even back when "he [Franklin] said he saw me [and declared] that's she's going to be my wife." She, on the other hand, wasn't yet ready to settle down: "I was just ready for the teenage life." The other experience was that mates were often bound together by the love and loyalty the women had paid to their men during times when the men suffered personal struggles with drugs, law enforcement, and unemployment.

That this experience was more common among those from the lower class is not surprising. Jonathan and Mariah Rowe were such a case; at the time we interviewed them, neither had graduated from high school. Mariah recalled sleeping on Jonathan's front porch with him through those nights when his mother refused to let him in because of his being high or drunk. Despite troubles such as these, the Rowes endured as a couple and eventually got married.

The Tompkins are middle class. Ava (who is from Bermuda and identifies as Caribbean) and Anthony (American-born black, but with Caribbean immigrant parents) met on a sports field where Anthony was being trained in college track and field and Ava served as an assistant coach. Anthony said that he could see right away that "Ava had her stuff together," and Ava had been eyeing the "cute athlete" on the field for some time. On the day Anthony first walked into her office, Ava said she knew he would be her husband: "God made it obvious to me." As soon as Ava's roommates moved out of her apartment, Anthony moved in. Because Ava's mother was a vehement opponent of cohabitation, Ava suggested that the two go ahead and get married fairly soon. That marriage took place one week later at the courthouse.

A carwash might be thought of as a highly unusual site for a relationship to begin. But a carwash is indeed where Trinidadian Francoise Everett and American-born black Bruce Everett met. The owner of the carwash was a mutual friend. It was only after Francoise was convinced that Bruce's "crush" on her was more than superficial that their one year of causal dating turned into something more serious. Francoise had expressed at that time that she really had not wanted be with someone younger than she was (and Bruce was *eight years* younger). This age difference was something she saw as inviting "unnecessary drama." Bruce, on the other hand, was not concerned. He was just happy to find things progressing nicely between them. The Everetts, from the working class, were engaged after only ten months of dating.

Jackson Lewis was the only Haitian among the spouses we interviewed, and Jasmine Lewis is an American-born black. They are a middle-class couple. Jasmine was not shy in letting us know that she had a lot of reservations about getting together with Jackson because of all the rumors about Caribbean men's infidelity. Kamala Kempadoo (2009), a professor of social science at York University in Toronto, says,

> Such arrangements are usually associated with men and considered to be an accepted part of (African) Caribbean masculine social life. ... Barrington Chevannes concludes that "becoming an African Caribbean man privileges one to engage in all ... forms of sexual relations, from the promiscuous and casual to multiple partnerships (which in effect is unrecognized polygamy)".[9] (9)

Jasmine Lewis further explained that she was really nervous about this issue from their first meeting all the way up to the non-church wedding in which they were married. It was her concern that "lots of families would be popping up" from relations Jackson might have with a number of different women. And she felt that Jackson simply expected her to accept his actions. We were not able to learn whether this problem ever actually materialized with the Lewises, but we did hear echoes of similar concerns among other women married to Caribbean men.

Kempadoo cautions us that the more holistic studies of Caribbean culture address sexuality as distinct from gender. That is, sexuality for both male and female Caribbeans is quite intricate, and infidelity is but one aspect of "a range of sexual arrangements and practices appreciated" (12)[10] in that region. Caribbean sexual practices, Kempadoo believes, should be understood as often distorted by the way the Caribbean is sold to the world as a sexually exotic tourist destination, exploited for pleasure of others "within local and global economies" (12).[11]

As this research began, we assumed that we would be collecting a number of details from our African study couples about the role their African heritage played in fashioning how the couples came together. And though both of us were fairly well acquainted with a number of African customs and folkways related to African marriage, such as arranged marriage and formal polygamy, we could not predict how prominent such cultural features would be among our contemporary immigrant African couples. As it turned out, their beginnings were similar in many ways to that of the other ethnic couples, with hints of a different flavor here and there where gender was concerned.

Simeon and Kalinda Goodman hail from Kenya. Kalinda was quick to let us know how strongly she feels about her "Mr. Right." She explained that when she first encountered Simeon, she could see that he was a "soft-spoken" man who allowed her to "speak her mind," both of which are attributes that she claimed were rare among Kenyan men: "they're usually more commanding." She was so taken by him early on that she forgot to ask whether or not he was a virgin. This was something a virgin like herself would have wanted to have known from the beginning. A Kenyan man not being a virgin would very likely indicate that he had had at least one child by another woman, something in which Kalinda did not seem to have any interest *at all*.

Travon and Abeni Sesay are Cameroonian and an African couple from the working class. The couple dated for just four months before they married. Travon explained that "it is not typical for couples to date for very long [in Cameroon]. We don't waste time, you know." They met on the East Coast while traveling and almost immediately determined that "everything just worked as one. We've been together ever since." Travon said he was attracted to Abeni because "she was different. She was the best (compared to other women). She was quiet. She would take care of me, you know." Abeni said she admitted that she was primarily attracted to Travon's physical appearance and demeanor: "His height. He was tall. He was handsome." But she also felt that he had a great personality, was quiet, and a hard worker: "Just compatible."

According to many sources, Africans are among the most educated groups immigrating to the United States.[12] Kenneth and Tracy Buckley, both from Sudan, exemplify that fact but are not typical of the African couples we met. Both spouses were successful in being accepted to institutions of higher learning here in the United States and in pursuing careers in health care. But they lamented feeling a bit unsettled among the people they had come to know, whose lifestyles and traditions were so different from what they were accustomed to back in Sudan. When the couple met, Kenneth was attending dental school at NYU and Tracy was completing her medical residency in Massachusetts. (They settled permanently in the United States after completing their programs of study.) It so happened that Kenneth received an invitation to a Sudanese wedding in Virginia—where he first settled in America—and there, he said, he caught the eye of a "good Sudanese woman," something he said was extremely difficult to find in the States.

What intrigued us most about the Buckley couple was that, unlike virtually every other African couple we met, their parents (back and forth from Africa) insisted on having a central role in their new relationship. Kenneth stated that Tracy's parents "demanded my presence, and I showed up and they wanted to know who I am. Just to know." Kenneth also knew there would be some specific rules he would have to follow if he was to someday marry Tracy. While he was not so surprised about this, he would have preferred a different arrangement. In addition to the African countries represented above, our research recorded marital-beginning narratives among those from Uganda, the Ivory Coast, and Sierra Leone as well, providing a rich dataset of experiences to ponder.

Andrew and Michelle, a newly middle-class white couple (their beginnings were more humble), met at her cousin's college. Michelle thought Andrew was "cute" at first sight, and he thought she "looked like Demi Moore," but he had a girlfriend at the time, so nothing transpired right away. Then the phone calls and lunches began, and before long love sprang, then a pregnancy, and finally a marriage.

Alex and Erin Larson were stationed at an Air Force base in Hawaii and lived in the same barracks. They were both confined to those barracks for official reasons at one point, making their frequent contact unavoidable. It was during that time that Alex became convinced, "Man, she wants me!" They "chased around each other" after that for about two years before becoming a couple. They are working-class white.

Jeff and Sue Ann Powell met in high school but didn't really notice each other much until they met again later at a community swimming pool. Turned out that the girl who he had recently broken up with was a friend of Sue Ann's at the time. Sue Ann had also recently ended another relationship. The two of them worked long hours during the week, so dating was sparse, and they broke up twice in the process. Still, they ended up moving in with each other after just one month: "[His mother] didn't want him coming out with me. He was, you know, he was his mommy's baby, so you know. Things weren't working out with his mom so, yeah, he moved in with me." They are lower-class white.

And then there are the Wilcoxes—Harold and Bethany—who met at a market near a local hospital where he sold pretzels and she would regularly buy iced tea. On their first date, she brought along four of her friends, just in case. They are working-class white.

The Dating Phase

The definition of dating that we employ for this research is the various interpersonal and social activities that two people engage in over time in order to move forward from their initial attraction to an intimate *relationship*. Courtship is where the dating is deliberately constructed with the goal of establishing a permanent intimate partnership (*marriage*). But because the associated rituals of modern courtship and dating look so similar, and because our study couples had already established marriages between them, we chose to use the term *dating* to encompass the full continuum of these activities.

Many factors influence mate selection, and this reflects a wide array of societal norms. These factors are embodied within two social theories on dating that we consulted and that seemed most relevant for this study of contemporary, 30-something African-American mates: Social Homogamy Theory and Free-Choice Mate Selection Theory. Social Homogamy Theory suggests that people are attracted to those whose social and cultural backgrounds align with theirs; with Free-Choice Mate Selection Theory, these backgrounds fade in influence against the pure attraction mates have to one another, the love they have for each other, and their desire to marry. Among our study couples, we see that their shared ethnicity (as we define it here) and social class status and background are highly significant to their beginning a relationship, but that allowing their relationship to form freely from everyday interactions is equally important.

Note that while the discussion in this chapter is divided into three different phases of African-American marital formation, no phase is entered into based on some concrete blueprint for what happens or how long each phase should last. Dating practices vary a great deal across the study couples, though much that goes on can be grouped into broad categories of what Pamela Braboy Jackson et al. (2011)[13] refer to as symbolic dating activities. These scholars consider "sexual intimacy, gifting, and family interactions" to be "potential markers of relationship seriousness."[14] But given that we could find no sociological investigation isolating *African-American* dating patterns, we made no assumptions about what important relationship markers we would find.

There are still those in modern society who prefer to adopt the more traditional, gendered model of dating where the man initiates the interaction, women look and act feminine, the couple rarely interacts spontaneously, parents have a good deal of say about things, and, most importantly, marriage is the only intended outcome of it all. But many couples now sketch things out as they go along and are very comfortable envisioning marriage as far off or working toward a cohabitation arrangement. Still others today, especially younger people, are likely to participate long-term in the popular "hook-up culture," the most casual of the dating types and primarily driven by the desire for sexual encounter. Our study offers nothing to suggest that this hook-up culture was of interest to the study couples.

American-born blacks Barry and Christine Adams married about seven years after they began dating. The two were only teenagers then; they met at a nightclub (we suppose that they used fake identification to enter that club) when he was a high school junior and a baseball player and she was a sophomore and a member of the marching band. After a while, the couple started interacting more outside of the club. Aside from attending the club, dating involved typical activities such as going to the movies and eating at restaurants. After a couple of years, they both dropped out of high school and had a child, which prompted them to move in together. At that time, Christine's mother was extremely helpful in caring for the baby; she would pick the child up from their home and keep him for two to three days at a time. Being periodically relieved from parenting duties helped the couple find various ways of making ends meet through odd jobs. Then, a second child was born within just a year or two. Barry decided the time had come for him to propose, so he surprised her with a ring.

Another American-born black couple who met when they were young is Charles and Keisha Parish (aged 15 and 19, respectively). They claimed the fact that they were "wearing the exact same shirt" let them know they would be together forever. But then Charles had to leave to begin his service in the United States Army. Before leaving, and perhaps in his mind to seal the deal between them, Charles told Keisha that he knew that she would soon become pregnant by him. Not long after he left, they had a baby daughter. Then, after their second child was born, Charles contacted Keisha and told her to go pick up a marriage license. He returned home a few days later, and they were married in a modest ceremony.

Marvin was still in high school when he met Jennifer at the nursing home where they both worked. The Johnsons (American-born blacks) recalled a very romantic evening they spent back then—attending his senior prom. Jennifer described that evening as "magical" because he treated her so well by opening doors for her, buying her a very nice meal, and taking her for a walk along the waterfront. The fact that Marvin owned a car made it easy for them to slip away on the weekends to vacation and to attend church on Sundays. They eventually started living together but soon had financial trouble, which led them to move back to their respective parents' homes, something they found agonizing. Within a week, they convinced their pastor to marry them in his office. A small family ceremony was held for them a few months later. They settled nicely into a middle-class existence.

Lamar and Thandi Albright (Trinidadian and Belizean, respectively) first met and briefly dated in middle school. There was at least one break-up after that, but for a good while they maintained a strong relationship. Then Thandi "became a Christian" and broke off the relationship because she had been told that Christians are "unevenly yoked" when they are in intimate association with unbelievers. They were both devastated by the separation. They moved on and dated other people for many years. Then, they regained their friendship when they enrolled in college at the same institution and found that there was something still "there" between them. Luckily for them, Lamar had become a Christian during the time they were apart. Lamar said he had a reassuring conversation with God about marrying her. The couple married in a medium-sized wedding at Thandi's godmother's house in upstate New York. Lamar said the wedding was "wonderful and intimate."

Gabriel and Taylor McCoy, both Caribbean, though from different islands, seemed to have gotten over the fact that their first meeting began with Taylor nearly bowling Gabriel over with her car! Jokingly, Taylor said, "[Nearly] run him over, yeah, yeah, I did. You know, scare him to death first and he'll know what he's dealing with." Their dating began by traveling together to the Northeast from Florida. After that, they "hung out every day." Taylor soon became pregnant. It was her first child and, "I was like, I'm not going to do it by myself." Gabriel agreed that she shouldn't go it alone, so they settled for a spell in Florida and had the baby. They had three more daughters, but Gabriel's two sons from two prior relationships have never lived with them. The McCoys are working class.

Odell and Kylie Velarde are the one Cuban couple we interviewed (she is black, he is not) and were the oldest couple, ages 54 and 39 respectively.[15] Odell said, "We have a beautiful relationship. We ignore the age difference. She doesn't see herself as a younger person. Sometimes it gets in the way, but it's no big deal. I love everything about her." What was hesitantly revealed over the course of this interview was that Odell had been married twice before. He stated that he was "more free" back then (meaning he could sleep with other women) because he was away working six days a week. At the time they met, Kylie had been looking for someone like Odell, "someone more old than me. It's normal [for Cubans]." She said she knew Odell was the man for her from the very beginning: "I enjoyed when we are together, when we [made] love."

Dating rituals among the African study couples were communicated more readily by them than by the other study couples, and their dating rituals were somewhat distinctive. For example, the dating period for Dre and Brianna Jamme (Ghanaian and American-born black, respectively) frequently involved Dre cooking traditional Ghanaian meals to help her better understand the man and the culture she chose. Their relationship began when the two were riding a bus and noticed that they both owned the same cell phone. She waited a couple of weeks before calling him, then the dating relationship took off. But Brianna admitted that she failed to ask him his name for the longest time: "I just called him 'Africa.'" Dre struggled to "get used to the American way of life," including Brianna's extremely busy social life—her going out with friends, to happy hours, and post-happy hours. He was stunned by "all that freedom" that both men *and* women in the United States enjoy. But he said he cared for Brianna so much that he regularly relaxed his traditionalism for her happiness and so that they could do many things together. He also loved that she was a generous person, helping him out financially now and again, even when that money was used in part to send money home to his family in Ghana.

When a friend encouraged young Danny Chebet to join the youth group at a Catholic church in Kenya, he did so right away knowing that this could be his opportunity to personally meet Alena. Alena Chebet was then an intriguing youth group leader who was even younger than 17-year-old Danny. Both mates had come from "very religious" families. Danny said that what he liked most about her was her "innocence, her naiveté." But what attracted her to him was that he was a bit of "a rebel," "exotic," "a bad boy making up his own rules in life." Danny was her first boyfriend and the only intimate partner she would ever have. They were together all the time. But she soon realized that she "had to step out of the teenage novel" way of thinking and acting and "step into the real world; this was real life." Danny took full advantage of the time he was able to spend with Alena when she would come home from college. He spoke passionately about the fact that he didn't want to share his love with anyone else and that he trusted Alena very much. They dated for five years and had a daughter before they married under pressure from their parents.

Jacob McAvoy (from the Ivory Coast) and white-American Emily (from Oregon) were co-workers in Ghana. While there, Jacob decided that he would help Emily improve her French-speaking skills. It was from within this arrangement that "love started." Eventually, Emily decided to return to the United States to begin graduate school. But she continued to visit and work in various regions of Africa and would almost always join with Jacob in doing so. The time came when they realized they needed to strongly consider whether they could "make a life together." Emily explained that while she understood that negotiating a bicultural relationship is difficult no matter what the two cultures are, she still wanted to clarify which of his family practices would be unacceptable to her should they decide to marry (such as requiring a future daughter to cover her head due to his being Muslim). Consensus on such matters took a great deal of work, but they must have found sufficient bicultural common ground. They married a short time later.

There was a second African and white-American study couple interviewed for this study, this one based in Senegal. Daniel Naki, who is from Cameroon, and Sophia met during a party organized by the international development company Sophia was working for at the time. Daniel was studying veterinary medicine and was "already integrated in Senegalese society," but Sophia was new to the country. It wasn't long after their relationship began that they started talking about the future. Daniel was not averse to getting married at some point, but it required that he ask her a number of questions to determine what she liked and disliked about his culture. He was quite impressed with the responses she eventually gave, and concluded, "she's an African with white skin." He could see that she had met his "goal" of finding a partner who understood him: "She was very open minded to all Senegalese culture and family."

After Joshua and Donna Jones (a white couple) met in their teens through his sister, they started dating right away. Joshua was pleased to learn that Donna was nothing like the girl he had recently been in a relationship with for two years. They went on their first date to the movies the day after they met. Their dating life was quickly curtailed because on the day after going to the movies, Donna moved in with Joshua's family due to the family strife she was suffering at home. Then, in another quick turn-about, Joshua's mother got fed up with the housing arrangement and forced him to make a choice between her and Donna. He chose Donna. In time, the couple found jobs at a local restaurant and made ends meet. Their closeness led them to realize that this was the first time either of them had ever really felt loved: "[we] didn't have love in our family lives."

Allen Kennedy's grandfather is credited with having brought his bartender grandson and Meredith together. Meredith had known Allen's grandfather since she was a child. After he pressed Allen twice to take her phone number, the relationship got on its way: "we went on a date, and we went on another date, and another date and …". The two never described the details of these dates but talked of them with pleasure. The dating went on for nine months and then Meredith made it clear: "she said she was behind on her *plan*." Marriage plan. She had wanted to be married and have a child by then (age 22). The couple is middle class.

The last of these three white couples are also middle class—Richard and Pamela Taylor. The Taylors had complex romantic relationships with others on the side during the early weeks of their relationship. After Richard and Pamela had encountered each other for the first time, they arranged to meet regularly for visits at each other's homes, which is what Richard meant when he said, "we just started dating." Pamela said she would always remember that on one of their early dates, Richard became ill from some spaghetti he had eaten at his grandmother's earlier that day. They were only 16 years old when all of this started; he went to public school and she went to Catholic school. They made the most of their weekends; that was when most of their relationship rituals took place. Richard repeated, "we just started dating and couldn't get rid of one another." Apparently, the couple did not find it contradictory that they "[broke] up a couple of times" and at the same time "could not get rid of each other." Still, Pamela was clearly smitten with Richard: "I didn't want somebody that was running all the time, like (going) to clubs. I didn't want any of that stuff. I sort of knew that I wanted to see if this relationship would work. And it did."

The Transition to Marriage

In his book *The Marriage-Go-Round: The State of Marriage and Family in America Today*, sociologist Andrew Cherlin discusses the sweeping changes that occurred over the twentieth century and finds it fascinating that

> at a [contemporary] time of great public concern about the supposed decline in marriage, it's remarkably high. … [T]he real puzzle is not why there is so little marriage but why there is so much of it. In short, why does anyone bother to marry anymore?[16] (136)

Despite popular imagery and the many real challenges they face as ethnic minorities, African Americans clearly are counted among those who regularly bother to marry—who choose to mark off their adult family life with this "capstone" (139). A recent Pew Research analysis of Current Population Survey data found that "while Blacks are more likely than whites to have never been married (and less likely to be currently married), a much higher share of Blacks (58%) than whites (44%) say that it's very important for a couple to marry if they plan to spend their lives together."[17] Thus, whether the initiation of a dating relationship is ushered in by friends or by pure chance; whether the solidification of said relationship occurs over a brief or prolonged period of dating; whether difficult personal circumstances lead to deep, empathic bonding; or whether an intimate couple faces the headwind of dissimilar cultural heritage, many African Americans will crown these experiences by choosing to legally marry. In doing so, they agree to enter into a public commitment of "enforceable trust" (138)[18]—an optimistically lifelong investment in shared love, financial solvency, and unadulterated pleasure.

In this section we examine the varying degrees of deliberateness with which the African-American dating relationships turned toward marriage, and whether these variations reflect ethnic and/or class distinctions. Traditionalism lies at one far end of this continuum; what lies at the other is hard to name and characterize. But what is clear is that these study couples knew that marriage was what they felt they needed in order to move forward, though not everyone was sure that this was the right decision in retrospect.

We could not help but notice that of the sixty-one couples we interviewed for this study, no fewer than twenty-eight (about 46%) chose to get married at a *courthouse* by a justice of the peace. African Americans were more likely to choose the courthouse wedding than the other three study groups. Because only one couple stated that this choice was made to avoid the cost of a more formal wedding, the argument cannot be made that the African Americans were swayed by economic issues. Most other couples chose a formal or informal wedding in a church building, some small and some big, some "quick," one "nice and sassy," and another attracting friends and family members from all over the world.

American-born black Eric Varner said that he and Diamond, a working-class couple, dated for nine long years, and had met at ages 17 and 15. Eric hounded Diamond to marry him for some time, until he wore her down and she accepted his proposal. He said that that he really couldn't detect any difference in their relationship once they were married. While the couple saw dating and marriage as different "phases in life, learning experiences," they ultimately describe these phases as merely parts of a whole. Their older two daughters were born before they married, and the third child, a surprise, was conceived after. Diamond said it's funny that *any* of this even happened: she never thought she would ever get married. But get married they did. But when we asked the Varners about their wedding, neither could recall very much, not even who had attended.

Adam and Netra Gardner, also American-born blacks, knew each other in middle school; he had a huge crush on her. Then they met up again in their early- to mid-20s. Netra again gave him the runaround, this time for about three months. But that reunion helped Adam to finally work up the nerve to ask Netra out on a date. The decision to marry was also delayed by this and that, but Adam and Netra finally got married at the courthouse with just family present: "About 25 people each." A big reception followed. Netra said they decided to marry because "[they] just wanted to be with each other, and [they] didn't feel like there was any reason to be with anybody else." They continued living in the home they had shared for a while and in which they had raised the baby born four months before the wedding. Each of them also had children from previous partners. Netra's oldest son was 5 when they started their bona fide relationship, and Adam's oldest son was 3. "[The children] have been together most of their lives ... we raised them together."

It was one of Emmett Smith's female college classmates who orchestrated things so that he could meet Denise a second time, and hopefully with more success. That meeting happened at the end of one of their classes. As it turned out, the two both majored in social work. Denise admitted that she didn't see anything special about Emmett when they began their friendship:

I figured this is how all the guys act, so I really didn't think too much into it. But as things settled down and I got a little more comfortable with the environment and could observe him, I liked what I saw. I could see he was a very nice person.

The decision to marry ultimately came about this way. Denise claimed that during one particular summer when Emmett vacationed with his male friends, he seemed make up his mind about her becoming his wife. When Emmett returned, Denise found a ring in the souvenir bag he brought home. Their whole process took about five years. Denise was also pregnant by then. Things culminated with a courthouse wedding— "She didn't want to wobble down the aisle"—surrounded by a good number of friends and family members. They are American-born black.

Among the Caribbean couples are James Davis and community college-grad Mia Davis, who are barely hanging on financially despite Mia's education. This couple began dating immediately—two days after they met—and then moved in together just a short while after that. James said he knew: "God supplied me with a good woman. She was the one." He said that his main motivation for getting close to Mia was to have a woman in his life—someone he would marry—to help him "stay out of trouble" (a theme revealed earlier). The loss of his mother and father led him into fights with other guys, and he was in and out of jail for selling drugs. James was married once before, and it was she who was charged at that time with keeping him out of trouble. In fact, he and this woman got engaged when he was in prison. The couple had divorced about four years earlier, before he met Mia, and he had children from that and other relationships. But once he met Mia, he put all his bets on her.

Medical issues nearly destroyed the Trotters' relationship before it really ever began. Both Ryan and Samantha developed serious illnesses not long after they met. Samantha (born to a Jamaican mother and a Guyanese father) had to have surgery, and Ryan (American-born black) developed Type I diabetes. The couple is middle class. Once the decision was made to get married, the Trotters saw that pre-marital counseling was in order, so they arranged it. Ryan thought that Samantha had "big issues with blame." In particular, she blamed his mother for not guiding him so as to prevent diabetes when he was young. There had also been a lot of petty arguing between them. The "toughest patch," as they called it, was during their 18-month engagement. Their long engagement was criticized by a number of acquaintances, but the Trotters saw taking their time as a way of limiting risk in their relationship. They conveyed how proud they were to have stuck by each other throughout these tough times. They eventually married at the courthouse and did not plan to start a family for several years.

Working-class couple Dixon and Shenice Ryan (American-born black and Trinidadian respectively) got married because Shenice became pregnant with their daughter. They wanted their daughter to have an "actual family, not just a mommy and a daddy." They were already living together, but cohabiting as parents just didn't jibe with their family values. Dixon saw marriage as a binding contract with someone who he could confide in without any fear of betrayal. Shenice was originally attracted to Dixon's "charming ways." She said that she used to work at a local McDonald's and he would come in frequently on his lunch break. He worked at a nearby printing shop up the street. She was 17 and he was 21 at the time. Shenice first brought up the idea of marriage; they both got solidly on board after she became pregnant. The baby was about a year old where they married at the courthouse.

Among the African couples was Rahim Yabu (from Sierra Leone) and Joyce Yabu. Rahim immigrated to the United States in hopes of continuing his university studies but was prevented from doing so because of what he said was "the poor economy here." Soon after arriving, Rahim met Joyce (an American-born black divorcé) through Joyce's mother, who was his co-worker. The mother's matchmaking turned out to be quite productive. Love came at first sight. The couple decided to get married a short time later, but not, they say, simply because Joyce got pregnant. They married in a courthouse. (Joyce said she would have preferred a marriage ceremony in a more intimate space.) Unfortunately, the Yabu marriage quickly took a difficult turn. When we interviewed Joyce, we learned the couple was living in separate residences. Joyce admitted she kicked him out of the house after an argument a couple of months before. Rahim's interview revealed that Joyce, a rape survivor, was suffering from severe bipolarism, and Rahim was emotionally tapped out. Further, to his dismay, neither spouse had yet secured a decent job.

Isaiah and Makayla Scott met in high school and then wound up attending the same university and taking classes together in Uganda. After she finished college, Isaiah recommended that Makayla secure a teaching job, as he had. As a result, they were able to see each other more often, like when she would make dinner for Isaiah and they would participate in a number of leisure activities together. Isaiah was sure to give her "little gifts," something commonly expected in Uganda and other African countries. A couple of years or so later, Isaiah returned from a conference in the United States to find that Makayla was pregnant. She explained, "Not being married at that time, it was not going to be a good thing." As is customary in their culture, the two families were immediately introduced to each other. Isaiah told us that he strongly embraced a folk notion he was taught: "Know the person you will marry. Date for a long time, and preferably if you decide to marry, take a second look." Despite pregnancy and motherhood, Makayla continued to attend a number of different U.S. graduate schools, often joining up with her husband. The two were well on their way to the middle class.

One of the most significant observations we made among the white study couples was scarce among the others. In general, the white couples saw getting married as the logical and right thing for people of their age to do. They strongly suggested that by the time one reaches his or her 30s, he or she should be stable educationally and economically. And soon after, one should identify an intimate mate and engage in some form of dating. If these mates desire to have children, getting pregnant would be the next logical step. Finally, getting married—either before or after children are born—should be simple and should involve only those closest to the couple. A number of the white spouses stated that marriage is "just something you do," and they had simply decided to do what was expected of them. Thus, the white study couples seemed intent on letting us to know that they were well-schooled in traditional marriage ideals and that they sought to maintain them. Their traditional ideals were not always evident in their enactment of intimate relationship, however.

Lynn and William Brown—like so many of their peers—woke up one day during their early dating phase and found that she was pregnant.

They met each other at ages 16 (still in high school) and 23, respectively, and made sure to "keep (their) relationship on the down-low" for just a while from the parents. Lynn said that when they first met, "he was already talking about marriage and kids, and it kind of threw me off"; but in short order she "just let go" and followed his lead. Once Lynn's baby bump began to peek through, they thought they should inform the parents that things were about to change in a big way. Given that her daughter was set on having a child with William, Lynn's mother, a tax preparer, helped William to file an annulment from his daughter's mother and get his finances in order. At the time of our interview, William was seeing this daughter every weekend. The couple made a point to state that their first child was "planned" and that this was grounds for their getting married. Lynn married William (in a courthouse), had their daughter, and graduated high school all in the same year.

From their interview transcript and other data that were collected, we found not one mention of "love" between Michael and Melanie Greene, as was the case with other white study couples as well. The Greenes (a working-class couple) were highly pragmatic in thinking through the option to marry. They described "negotiating" with one another in determining exactly how everything should proceed. As members of the Jehovah's Witness faith, they also sought to order their steps toward marriage as they had been taught to do, though they never explained what they practiced in their relationship that was Jehovah's Witness in nature. It all appeared very neat and tidy. But while they certainly seemed to respect each other and care about the marriage, we gained no sense of how they felt toward one another as intimate partners.

Laura Thompson said that she was so glad to not have to date anymore once she and Mike Thompson solidified their relationship. She was certain that she was moving toward a comfortable and solid marriage that was built upon the same ideal as her parents':

> My father always worked, my mother never worked … You know, [the husband] should go out and support his family and the wife should stay at home and do everything she can to support her husband. It's just how I know most families don't do it that way these days.

Mike and Laura were certain that arranging a marriage in this way was the only way is should be done. Mike described Laura as his "photo negative": he considered them complete opposites, making way for them to ultimately be the perfect partners for their form of marriage. They ended up being married in a small, intimate wedding officiated by a priest, witnessed by a volunteer from that church, and attended by "just a few friends." Though of lower class, they did not speak of any socioeconomic difficulties during the early phases of their relationship.

Budding Black Relationships

These stories of marital beginnings are indicative of those told across our study couples. The distribution of social class status differed somewhat across the four ethnic groups, yet social class appears to have only been mildly correlated with the couples' relationship trajectories. What we found most evident as an influence of social-class status were the locations where the couples first met and dated—in college, for example, versus in their neighborhood or in or around the military. That is, social-class status often dictated where opportunities for relationship formation took place. On the other hand, while many of the elements of the transition to marriage cut across ethnic lines, the stories as a whole tend to organize in interesting ways by ethnic group.

Where the white study couples were generally less forward about affection (love) and seemed more committed to espousing a traditional ideology regarding the appropriate path to married life (though their support of traditional marriage rarely fit with their actual process), American-born black and Caribbean immigrant couples included numerous terms of endearment in describing their mates, and they showed little concern for the fact that they had cohabited or bore children before they married. For both of these ethnic groups, many wives emphasized that what they required most from a mate were things like decency, goodness, friendship, and monogamy. And many African immigrant husbands and wives explained that they selected their mate primarily because he or she shared their native values and traditions yet demonstrated the ability to relax traditional marriage expectations to make the relationship work.

Couples across the ethnic spectrum described specific and significant challenges that they had to face in the course of building their relationships. Several native-born black couples were, at least for a time, troubled by law enforcement, drugs and alcohol, and unemployment dilemmas. Health issues were also frequently raised. The relatively higher social-class status that African immigrants as a whole held helped them to not fall prey to such issues. On the other hand, some found that their immigrant status limited their access to job and educational opportunities. And Africans' adjustment to life in the United States—particularly in finding a mate who they could relate to from their native country—was at times frustrating. The issue of male infidelity was raised here and there by the study wives. It seemed to be a stronger theme among the Caribbeans, though at least one African wife (Kenyan) said that infidelity is more common in Kenya than in the United States. In America, she said, life is so hectic that her husband has no time to cheat.

These stories of contemporary black marriage lay a foundation for examining how both positive and negative elements of these budding relationships flowed into married life once it was established. In the chapters that follow, we focus this examination on the gendered nature of black relationships once marriage occurs. We also explore how parenting is conceived and practiced among black families and how social forces both internal and external to black marriage shape black marital life. In each instance, we rely on the body of sociological theorizing and research to help inform our understanding of the marital lives these black couples experience.

Notes

1 When referring to "race" anywhere in this text, we lay no claim to it being real, but, rather, proclaim—as do most sociologists—that it is a sociallyconstructed and destructive concept created by dominant social powers to justify inequality among people of varying descent.
2 Of course, miscegenation was also illegal for whites until this time.
3 According to numerous sources, secular and religious, courtship is entered into with the intent to secure a marriage partner, where dating does not necessarily have such intentions.
4 Kent, Mary Maderios. 2007. "Immigration and American's Black Population." *Population Bulletin* 62(4):3–16.
5 For another discussion of how blacks (specifically degreed black women) enter and maintain romantic relationships, see Clarke, Averil Y. 2011. *Inequalities of Love: College-Education Black Women and the Barriers to Romance and Family.* Durham, NC: Duke University Press.

6 See Chapters 1 and 2 in Coleman, Marilyn, and Lawrence Ganong. 2003. *Points and Counterpoints: Controversial Relationships and Family Issues in the 21st Century.* Los Angeles, CA: Roxbury Publishing Co.

7 Cacioppo, John T., Stephanie Cacioppo, Gian G. Gonzaga, Elizabeth L. Ogburn, and Tyler J. VanderWeele. 2013. "Marital Satisfaction and Break-ups Differ Across On-line and Off-line Meeting Venues." *The Proceedings of the National Academy of Sciences* 110:10135–10140. Retrieved June 15, 2017 (www.pnas.org/content/110/25/10135. full.pdf).

8 Lewis, Kevin. 2016. "Preferences in the Early Stages of Mate Choice." *Social Forces* 95:283–320.

9 Kempadoo, Kamala. 2009. "Caribbean Sexuality: Mapping the Field." *Caribbean Review of Gender Studies: A Journal of Caribbean Perspectives in Gender and Feminism* 3:1–24. Barry Chevanes' quotes are from his 2001 book, *Learning to Be a Man: Culture, Socialization and Gender Identity in Five Caribbean Communities.* Kingston, Jamaica: The University of the West Indies Press.

10 Kempadoo, 2009.

11 Kempadoo, 2009.

12 See, for example, Pew Research Center. 2005. "6 Key Findings about Black Immigration to the U.S." Retrieved April 3, 2017 (http://www.pewresearch.org/fact-tank/2015/04/09/6-key-findings-about-black-immigration/).

13 Jackson, Pamela Braboy, Sibyl Kleiner, Claudia Geist, and Kara Cebulko. 2011. "Conventions of Courtship: Gender and Race Differences in the Significance of Dating Rituals." *Journal of Family Issues* 32(5):629–652.

14 Jackson et al., 2011.

15 We included the Velardes in the Caribbean sample given that at least one of them was still in their thirties.

16 Cherlin, Andrew. 2009. *The Marriage-Go-Round: The State of Marriage and the Family in America Today.* New York: Alfred A. Knopf.

17 Pew Research Center. 2014. "Record Share of Americans Have Never Married." Retrieved March 9, 2017 (http://www.pewsocialtrends.org/2014/09/24/record-share-of-americans-have-never-married/).

18 Cherlin, 2009.

4

MEN AND WOMEN, HUSBANDS AND WIVES

NEW PERSPECTIVES ON EGALITARIANISM

Terrell Glasser, an American-born, middle-class black husband, is waiting for Destiny and their two children. Terrell came off his latest 24-hour shift at the fire department and has tidied up their large, modern kitchen with its brightly painted walls and long, central island counter. After finishing her shift as a bookkeeper for a real estate broker, Destiny went shopping and picked up their son and daughter from elementary school. Now she rounds their SUV into their suburban housing development and pulls up to the curb of their three-story brick townhouse. The kids charge into the foyer with backpacks and plastic sacks of groceries, and Terrell hurries to help. Someone drops a bottle of soy sauce, and he runs back to the kitchen for rags. Destiny skirts the puddle, her arms loaded with more plastic sacks. Everyone assembles in the kitchen. The kids pull out their notebooks and sit at the long granite counter to begin their homework while Destiny and Terrell put away food. "What does organic mean, anyway?" Terrell asks Destiny, holding up a loaf of organic whole grain bread. "It means it doesn't have preservatives," she says, and he shrugs. They begin discussing what to prepare for dinner.

Sociologists of earlier generations proposed that dividing labor between husbands and wives was beneficial, natural, and essential to a functioning society. Emile Durkheim argued that separate marriage roles for men and women created "conjugal solidarity," bringing husbands and wives closer together, and that marriages like these were a model for the different roles people played in a community.[1] Having specific roles increased people's dependence on each other and thus made people bond together because they needed each other. The parts people played created a community in the way that a heart, liver, and other organs create a functioning body.

In mid-twentieth-century America, functionalists such as Talcott Parsons argued that the greater good of society depended in part on husbands and wives having different roles in families, with women playing an expressive (nurturing) role and men playing an instrumental role (breadwinner).[2] In the 1970s, economist Gary Becker connected separate roles for husbands and wives to marital success, both financially and socially. In the language of economists, he suggested that having two roles, one based at home and the other in the workforce, allowed couples to "maximize their utility"; in other words, having separate specializations helped couples to be richer and happier.[3]

None of these descriptions fit Destiny and Terrell's family at all. Both work, both take care of their children, both cook dinner. Sometimes they take turns and sometimes they work together, but they work as a team. But not so long ago, ideas about the roles of husbands and wives became so embedded that when women did not want to be wives and mothers, or did not want to put their own wants and needs second to their husbands' and children's, psychologists identified them as immature and even mentally ill.[4] Are Destiny and Terrell an example of the new egalitarianism, a modern couple living according to new, modern values? Or have some couples always lived this way, flying under the radar of social scientists because they didn't fit the mold—and because ideas about families were rarely based on the patterns of black families such as Destiny and Terrell's?

Marriage, Race, and Employment

Social theories did not play out well for black wives—or husbands—in the first seven decades of the twentieth century. More than a quarter of black wives were working in "gainful occupations" in 1900, but a mere 3% of white wives were. At the same time, more than 90% of black and white husbands were working. The gap gradually narrowed, but it didn't close until the 1990s, when nearly two-thirds of both black and white wives were working, a trend that has remained more or less the same up to the present. Despite what social scientists have said about women entering the workforce and its impact on families, Destiny and Terrell's work patterns are not really a "new" normal but one that has been there all along—especially among black families.

Some scholars believe that the long history of black wives holding jobs outside the home has led to more egalitarian relationships between black spouses.[5] Others have suggested that wives working, and the power that paid employment gives them within marriage, are the main causes of decreasing rates of marriage among blacks and prevent the formation of stable, nuclear families.[6] Black families, on the other hand, have often seen the money a woman brings home as part and parcel of her role as a wife and mother,[7] unlike white families, who more often feel that a wife's work takes away from being a good wife and mother. Certainly, neither Destiny nor Terrell ever said anything about Destiny's work being a problem—nor did they talk about it being a benefit. They didn't really talk about it at all, other than the fact that she works a typical schedule in her office job, while Terrell works 24-hour shifts that can occur any day of the week, but is then often at home for days at a time. Her job is just an expected component of everyday life, not a conflict with family, and certainly not a subject for moral debate.

The increasing rate of women in the workforce generally, and of white, middle-class wives and mothers in particular, has been accompanied by an overall increase in men's contributions to housework and childcare.[8] A majority of younger couples, similar in age to those in our study, now express a desire for egalitarianism in their relationships.[9] Though our society has not completed a full-fledged gender revolution, in which there is no distinction between men and women's roles in the home or in the workforce,[10] most people generally assume that American marriage is progressing from a "traditional" model to a more "egalitarian" one.[11] There are two problems with this assumption. One is that the hallmark of "traditional" marriage has generally been the gendered division of labor prevalent in white, middle-class marriages from industrialization to the 1970s, which was not necessarily the case for many black families. The other is that scholars, pundits, politicians, and the public at large have difficulty coming to any consensus about what it means to be egalitarian. Although Terrell and Destiny both work and contribute to housework and childcare in ways that most people would call egalitarian, their actions and values do not always line up, at least not in the way that social scientists would expect.

Egalitarian Values and Practice

Egalitarianism can apply to many roles in marriage, including parenting, employment, and interpersonal and educational roles.[12] Definitions of egalitarian marriage include equal economic and household contributions, complete role sharing, equally sharing in surplus benefits generated by the marriage, equal balance in who gets his/her way, gaining equally from the relationship, or equal bargaining power.[13] Some scholars combine measures, such as role sharing and equal decision-making power;[14] a balance of contributions to both housework and mental labor;[15] or equality in power, paid and unpaid labor, and love.[16]

Couples in our study, even those like Destiny and Terrell who shared breadwinning and housework, rarely used the term "egalitarian." They did, however, state ideals of having both spouses contribute equally to income earning, housework, and child-rearing. Generally, couples who held these ideals called them "sharing," "fairness," or contributing "fifty–fifty." Barry and Christine Adams, a lower-class, American-born black couple who are raising four children in Barry's father's basement, wanted to share responsibility for their household and family. Jobs that pay a living wage for them are in short supply, especially since neither finished high school. They both do what they can—Christine earns some money through babysitting, but Barry has chronic health problems stemming from a construction accident. He is in and out of the hospital, but he is not eligible for worker's compensation because he was not a full-time, regular employee when he got hurt. Both parents wind up being home a lot, whether they want to be or not. When asked about who does housework, they offered a lively discussion:

Barry: Well, with chores and everything, we share that.
Christine: Yeah, we share that, we do that with each other.

Barry: Because sometimes she tired and sometimes I'm tired.
Christine: Yeah.

They don't express egalitarianism as a political or religious ideology, but as an issue of teamwork and respect.

Among the American-born, black couples in general were most likely to be egalitarian in both action and attitude, especially if they were not religious. Among white couples, egalitarian values were most often expressed among middle-income spouses. When asked about an ideal marriage, Richard Taylor, a middle-class white father of two with a state government job, told us:

> The main thing is to take care of one another. Things shouldn't be assigned; things fall into place. Nothing is perfect, but [spouses] help one another. For example, with work—whoever gets off work first gets the kids, it depends. Some days he cleans, some days she does.

Egalitarians, whether black or white, American-born or immigrant, generally acknowledged that there might be times in the marriage when one member of the couple needs to contribute more to either breadwinning or homemaking. Allowing things to "fall into place" had to be accompanied by valuing fairness and equality.

Spouses did not always share an ideology. In fact, some women married to men who wanted to share childcare and household tasks engaged in "gatekeeping."[17] These wives wouldn't allow their husbands to either share or take charge of anything they thought wives and mothers should do. When their husbands tried, they were met with criticism—taking too long to fold laundry, putting silverware in the dishwasher the wrong way, or not dressing a child warmly enough. At the same time, gatekeeping wives often complained about the burden of being in charge.

In other cases, just because couples said they had egalitarian ideals did not mean they put them into practice. Joyce Yabu, an American-born black woman, and her husband Rahim, an African immigrant, are a working-class couple who said that they believe strongly in egalitarianism. Rahim emphasized, "Marriages are fifty–fifty," and that "the way we do things, if we are capable of doing certain things, we do it." He said work should not be divided by gender. Joyce agreed that responsibilities should be split "fifty–fifty." Because they agree, and because their house appears tidy and their children well cared for, it seems like they must live in a happy, egalitarian household. But when we talked to Joyce alone, a different story emerged:

> [I]t's me doing everything, cleaning the house, steam-clean—I steam-clean my floors, he does it once in a blue moon, but I steam-clean mine, so I bought my own thing, I wipe my own windows. … I can't do the outside, but I do the inside. I do dust. Certain stuff he just don't do when he come home. He goes straight—take his shoes off, plop right there on that couch right there on that big blue one and stretch out, and uh … the girls will be surrounding him, I have stuff to do in the bedroom, I'm between the bedroom and the kitchen, I'm doing stuff, twenty-four–seven. Yeah.

Their conflict has become intense enough that they are currently living separately.

These stories of being equal in word but not deed are shared among black and white couples alike. Candy and Ethan Springfield, a working-class white couple, insisted during their joint interview that they contribute equally in their relationship. Candy, an office manager, said, "I think it should be fifty–fifty no matter what." Ethan, who is currently unemployed but is working on a college degree online, added, "Right. I think that anything less than fifty–fifty, there's going to be some kind of problems." At the time of the interview, however, even though Ethan has been home all day, the house is cluttered, with dishes piled in the sink. Ethan's unemployment has stretched several months, but their daughter Dana is still attending a daycare near Candy's workplace. A month after the interview, Candy wrote an impassioned entry in her marriage diary, explaining that while Ethan was currently home all day, most of the family work still fell to her:

> He doesn't clean, and I am not talking about spotless cleaning here … He doesn't start dinner, and all he seems to do is watch

tv/movies and play video games ... I am just soooo beat and then in the morning he can't even get up with us and that makes me sad sometimes so I have to fix lunches for me and Dana and have to include a breakfast for Dana, it's just so hard.

Sociologist Pepper Schwartz refers to couples like Rahim and Joyce or Ethan and Candy as "near peers"—those who want to think of themselves as egalitarian but can't seem to make equality happen in real life.[18] They live their lives in the shadow of social expectations and power dynamics that let men off the hook at home and leave women to pick up the household scut work.

Sometimes there were subtler flaws in a couple's egalitarian story. Ryan Trotter, a middle-class, American-born black husband, shares housework with his wife Samantha, a Caribbean immigrant. In general, they are both content with their division of labor. Ryan emphatically rejects the bread-winner–homemaker dichotomy his parents practiced, and he is eager for Sam, who quit a job she hated, to resume working. At the same time, he is concerned that Sam's next job could increase her earnings far beyond his. He said, "I'm comfortable within reason, but I think if it ever got to be too much of a gap, then I'd be like, 'Oh, I got a [problem].'" Ryan doesn't think Sam would hold it against him if she earned more than he did, but he does not want to entertain the possibility. He is concerned with society's perceptions: "Someone could find out, well, your girl makes $30,000 more than you." Ryan has no concerns about out-earning Sam—his egalitarian ideal is only threatened if she has more economic power.

Conservative Values in Black and White

The literature tells us that although black men are generally more positive than white men about their wives' workforce participation, they are more conservative than white men on other attitudes regarding gender and marriage.[19] For black husbands, however, conservative values do not center on women's employment. Black husbands with "traditional" attitudes are as likely as egalitarians to have wives who work full-time, while traditional white men are more likely to have wives who work part-time or not at all.[20] Black wives with a "conservative" husband are actually more likely to work outside the home than are wives whose husbands' values are more liberal—the opposite is true for white wives.

A number of families in our study expressed conservative attitudes regarding marriage and gender roles, but among the American-born, there were strong distinctions by ethnicity. Traditional ideals based primarily on a breadwinning husband and a homemaker wife and mother were far more commonly expressed among whites than any black group. For whites, this ideology accompanied a desire to adhere to patterns they had observed growing up and a belief that children were best off if their mother did not hold an outside job. This view was often expressed as the proper order of things. Harold Wilcox, who encouraged his wife to quit her job once he made enough money to support their family, explained the ideal marriage: "Husband goes out and works, wife stays home and takes care of the kids, and that's it. It's the American way. It's the American old-fashioned way."

Rather than stressing breadwinning and homemaking as gendered spheres, American-born African-American couples often emphasized patriarchy in the form of male "headship" and offered religious justifications for male and female roles—roles that rarely had anything to do with employment or housework. Religious American-born black couples frequently asserted that the Bible states that the husband should be head of the household—but for them this applied to final decision-making power, not being a sole or primary breadwinner. American-born black women who expressed a belief in different marital roles for men and women usually held paid jobs and explained role differentiation in terms of male headship and—just as importantly—female submission, terms that were never mentioned among whites.

Among whites, traditional values usually lead fathers to work more and spend less time at home with their families.[21] In contrast, among American-born black wives we interviewed, an emphasis on male headship was a way to draw men home and make them more involved in family life. As Jennifer Johnson, an American-born black wife, said of running a household, "Black women today want to be the power woman," but it's important for them to "give [men] a chance." This emphasis on a patriarchal ideology often worked to make marriages more egalitarian in practice.

Early in Destiny and Terrell's marriage, Terrell left all of the decision-making to Destiny. He loved to wear the latest styles, drive a new car, and show off their new television to friends. Destiny managed their money, a task Terrell was happy to leave to her—she was a bookkeeper, after all. But Destiny didn't want to disappoint Terrell when he wanted something new, no matter how expensive it was, and she certainly didn't want to confront him about their worsening finances. In order to keep him happy, she let him do what he wanted, buy what he wanted, and go where he wanted while she picked up all the household tasks. As Terrell went his own way, Destiny could no longer control the wreckage, and the couple fell into bankruptcy. They lost their home, and they each moved back in with their parents. They weren't sure whether their marriage would survive. But both are devoutly religious, and they turned to their church for solutions. Each met with church elders, who guided them through Scripture to find a new path for their relationship, one that made Terrell the head of the household. Destiny explained that following the edicts of their church is the key to making their marriage work now:

> [T]hat was a commitment that I made to God. That I was going to be married to this man and respect him as the head. I would say when we try to follow that closely, the problems are less. It's when we try to do it our own way and not really following the reminders that we get from the Scriptures—that's where our problems come at.

Assigning Terrell the role of head of household and reinforcing this role through the institutional power of the church actually allowed their relationship to become more egalitarian. Destiny stepped back from taking on the bulk of household responsibilities, including responsibilities for managing all of their finances. Terrell needed to be at home spending time with her and the children in order to exercise his leadership, and he needed to understand their economic situation—and its limitations—in order to be the final decision-maker. Terrell agreed that biblical principles establishing him as head mandated his direct family involvement and had let the couple save their marriage and rebuild their lives.

While black couples frequently put biblical Scripture at front and center of their marriage values, among similarly devout white couples, religion was rarely—if ever—mentioned as influencing gender ideology or marital roles. Melanie Greene's husband, Michael, converted and joined her church when they married—the same church denomination as Destiny and Terrell's. Both are American-born whites, working class, and neither mentioned the concepts of headship or submission, but they do divide their household roles by gender. Michael feels he earns a haven through being the family's breadwinner, not that Melanie should provide one based on biblical principles: "I do the main part of the work, probably 99%, and I think I should come home and the house should be clean, and I think around dinner time she should do it." Although their religion supports gendered roles within marriage, they presented their division of labor in terms of personal values, not religious mandates, and they did not credit their religious beliefs for the success of their marriage.

Among black men from the lower class, some wished they *could* be breadwinners and believed that if they could bring home enough money, their wives would step back from work and create a haven for them. Even American-born black men sometimes longed for a "Leave it to Beaver"-type arrangement usually seen as a hallmark of white suburbia in the 1950s. For Bart McAllister, an American-born black husband who is currently unemployed while his wife works full time, a "traditional" marriage seemed like a dream:

> I can work all day and come home and smell my potatoes frying, my steak cooking, and I know it's for me. You know, I can go shower or whatever, I know my favorite show will probably be there, and my slippers are in the living room. I can kick back and have a nice cold beer or whatever while unwinding the day. That's ideal for me.

Bart, who did not complete high school and does seasonal work in fair weather, is his family's caregiver, raising his son from a previous relationship and helping his wife's teenage sister with her new baby. His wife Lori works full time, year-round, with low pay and few benefits. His fantasy includes having someone cooking for him and an income high enough to buy steak—in the meantime, his family is waiting until after Christmas to turn on their heat.

Lower-income, American-born blacks such as Bart acknowledged that discrimination, over-incarceration, and a lack of blue-collar jobs with living wages made role flexibility a necessity and a so-called traditional lifestyle unobtainable for them. Adam and Netra Gardner, a working-class, American-born black couple, explained the difficulty in meshing reality with their own more traditional expectations. Adam said, "They always say the male should take care of the family as far as financially, but nine times out of ten the woman makes more money than the man." Netra added, "That's because a lot of our males honestly can't get good-paying jobs because of their history and their previous lifestyles and that kind of stuff." As has been true for many black couples throughout American history, the Gardners put aside traditional role beliefs to enact egalitarianism as a practicality. Being traditional became a value *"they* always say"—not something for black families like theirs.

Immigrants and Married Life in America

Some researchers have long suggested that studies of black married life should consider black ethnic differences, such as those created by immigration.[22] Indeed, we found that immigrants often did have different values and practices when compared to American-born blacks—or to black immigrants from other parts of the world. Black immigrants are more likely to be married than American-born blacks, with marriage rates comparable to those of American-born whites.[23] Among black immigrants in the United States, Africans are more likely to be married and their children more likely to live in a two-parent household than Caribbean immigrants.[24]

Caribbean culture is highly patriarchal—men are undoubtedly in charge in most families, and that's what most people expect. Married women don't have the same kind of freedom that married men do, and they are usually expected to tolerate their husbands' affairs and violence toward them.[25] Many marriages begin as what has been called common-law marriage but would now be better known as living together in a serious relationship—legal marriage generally happens only after the couple has children and has stayed together for years.[26] Women usually take care of housework and childrearing with little involvement from men, while men are expected to earn money and to step in as disciplinarians.[27]

Women are often expected to adhere to traditional Caribbean values even after settling in the United States.[28]

Many sub-Saharan African cultures offer little respect to wives until they become mothers,[29] but becoming a mother does not mean that a woman gets the power to make household decisions.[30] African families often operate quite differently in the city and the country. Cities are more westernized in approaches to marriages—closer to patterns in the United States—while people living in the country still follow traditional cultural practices.[31] Regardless of where they live, most African couples are members of extended families, and often women spend their time with their sisters, mothers, grandmothers, aunts, and female cousins, while men spend most of their time with other male family members.[32]

Among couples we spent our time with, Caribbean and African immigrants approached marriage and family life very differently once they settled in the United States. For African immigrants, working together as equals was a change necessary to adapt to American society. Regardless of what country they came from, African immigrants had followed strictly gendered roles in their home countries. The men were indisputably "in charge." American life, however, required flexibility. African-born couples, as well as immigrants who had an American-born spouse, frequently spoke of "adjusting" by giving up African conceptions of gender roles in marriage. As Alexis Hoffman, who immigrated from Ghana, noted, "[O]f course you have your ideals, and this is what you're going to do and this is how things are going to turn out, but it doesn't always turn out that way, living together, having to adjust to figure out how the two of you manage, and deal with issues …"

Many African immigrants embraced egalitarianism as a way to "adjust." Even when couples still felt someone needed to be "in charge," they no longer saw the man as the one who should always take on that role. Their language became much like that of Richard, the white husband who emphasized flexibility based on individual needs. Emmanuel Marshall, a middle-class black husband originally from Ethiopia, said,

> Someone has to be in charge. You know what, the roles might switch. It is not 50–50—I give a 100, and you give 100, and we

keep this thing moving. But you can't go into it and ask what percentage are you giving. Sometimes my load will be heavier than yours, or vice versa, and sometimes you have to pick up my slack, and I'll pick up yours.

Some men were happy to give up the responsibility of being in charge all the time. Travon Sesay, who emigrated from Cameroon and is working-class, married an American-born black woman, Abeni. She grew up in the rural South with parents who had breadwinner–homemaker roles, but with Travon she adopted a more egalitarian lifestyle. Like Barry and Christine Adams, Travon emphasized sharing and contrasted that to what his life would have been like in Cameroon. He said, "I cook, I clean. She cook, she clean. That is what I like about America, everything is shared. It is not like back home [where the husband] pay all the bills. He doesn't cook." While most couples retained some traditional practices, both African husbands and wives discussed positive aspects of "adjusting" to a more egalitarian society. Unlike Destiny and Terrell, who found greater equality by stepping into gendered roles, for Africans, finding a balance in American life meant stepping out of them.

In contrast to African immigrants, most Caribbeans, both women and men, embraced traditional roles and gender divisions. Their ideas about marriage roles were that they should be gendered, patriarchal, and based on Scripture. One working-class Caribbean wife compared Caribbean men to "kings" and Caribbean women to "slaves." Several spouses reported that domestic violence was tolerated in their home countries— one working-class Caribbean husband told us that "some women need a good beating" so that they would "know their place."

Unlike Africans, who felt adjusting to American life was essential and helped them to be happier, Caribbean spouses strongly resisted adjusting to American ideals, even when doing so seemed like it would make their lives easier. Caribbean spouses discussed the importance of division of household tasks into those for men and those for women and having the man be in charge as a Bible-based mandate. Like whites, Caribbeans also felt that they should live as their own parents and other family members had. Francoise Everett, a working-class Caribbean immigrant, is married to Bruce, an American-born black who willingly does housework, but she still feels she should play the role that would be expected of her in Trinidad: "I try to cook every day. I don't like it, but that's how I was raised."

Much like the social theorists we discussed at the beginning of this chapter, Caribbean couples expressed that different roles for men and women made marriage function properly. Taylor and Gabriel McCoy are Caribbean immigrants who met in the United States, and are barely hanging on as working class. Taylor noted that she was raised in a family of car mechanics, but she leaves car maintenance to Gabriel because it is a man's job. Gabriel said, "For something like going to the grocery store, I would not go grocery shopping. That's for her to do, you know what I'm saying? I'm not saying it's above me or below me, but it ain't really my thing." Even when roles were not working out in daily life, couples felt they had to stick with them, often explaining that they had to because of their religious beliefs. James and Mia Davis, working-class Caribbean immigrants with two young daughters, had money problems, in part stemming from child support James paid for several children he had before meeting Mia. Both James and Mia agreed that Mia was the better money manager. She was smart and ambitious, and she had a college degree that would allow her to get a well-paying job. Still, Mia's beliefs made her hold back and try to keep James in charge:

> In a perfect world, I wish he would just give me the responsibility [for providing and money management]. I don't want to take that responsibility away from him. Because as head of household, you still have to give [the husband] that respect. You know, that they would manage the finances properly ... I pray in hopes that one day he could get there.

In the meantime, the family spiraled deeper and deeper into debt.

A Spectrum of Values and Practices

While many assume that wives in middle-class families are the most likely to choose to be homemakers because they are most likely to be married to a man who earns a family-supporting wage, the reality is that the more educated a woman is, the more likely she is to work for pay.[33]

This trend is even more true for black women than for white women, but U.S. Department of Labor statistics do not consider whether women are American-born or not. Most of the better-educated women we spoke with were employed or were involuntarily unemployed, though a few had chosen to leave the workforce temporarily either to care for their families or because of poor health.

Determining differences among the values of poor, lower-class, and working-class couples we interviewed could be difficult when it came to gender and work. We know the values expressed by each couple, and valuing having a wife at home, especially if she was a mother, seemed to predominate among our most economically unstable couples. However, these families were often in a precarious financial state precisely because they tried to scrape by on the husband's income alone. If more of these women were working but wished they were not, valuing having a wife at home might have appeared more prominently among working-class couples. We also interviewed a number of couples in which the husband was at home, rarely by choice, because he couldn't find a job, a situation that also made a family more economically fragile. In black families, a husband's unemployment was frequently attributed to racial discrimination as well as a tight job market. Only one couple we interviewed, a middle-class couple with a highly educated white wife married to an African immigrant husband, valued having the husband at home as a homemaker and caregiver.

African and Caribbean immigrants generally came from families where women took care of the home and children while men earned money and spent much of their leisure time with other men. Men were in charge, and women submitted. For Caribbeans and African Christians, traditional ideals were also rooted in their reading of the Bible. Regardless of religion, in their home countries, Caribbean and African men and women often did not spend much time together, and fathers were often described as "dictators." Despite these similarities in their home countries, African and Caribbean immigrants had divergent approaches to life in the United States. Caribbean men often said they wanted to be like their fathers, and many Caribbean men and women wanted their marriages to be like their parents' relationships. Among the couples we interviewed, Caribbeans felt the most strongly that men and women should stick to certain tasks, as when Taylor McCoy said she grew up in a family of auto mechanics but left car repairs to her husband. Couples worked fiercely to have traditional relationships even when it stressed their families and their relationships. In contrast, African immigrants, especially African Muslims, "adjusted" to their new lives in America by becoming more egalitarian, with women taking on employment and men taking on domestic tasks. Africans were more likely to say that they did not admire their parents' relationships, especially when fathers were "dictators." Africans had divided loyalties: traditionalism was best for African life, but egalitarianism was better for life in America.

We might argue that being able to adjust is usually better, no matter what direction it goes. As Barry and Christine Adams noted, to share, to "do that with each other," often brings couples closer together than trying to depend on each other to do different tasks. In real life, traditional spouses, at least the ones who wanted relationships like those that Durkheim, Parsons, and Becker suggested were the foundation of happiness, had a hard time putting their values into practice. Traditional white and Caribbean women usually worked for pay at least some of the time; even those who said they were not "working" took up part-time paid work, such as babysitting or home-based sales. American-born black and Caribbean women who believed in submission found full-blown submission a challenge in daily life, and many of their husbands found acting as a household head to be challenging as well. Destiny and Terrell said Terrell was the head of the household, but what that really meant was that he was involved in the household. Unlike traditional men in Caribbean and African countries, who took being "in charge" as license to live their lives however they chose, for Terrell Glasser, being "in charge" meant he had to be much more involved in family life. For Destiny, "submitting" to Terrell as head didn't mean quitting her job, it meant stepping back to give Terrell a space to fill. Once he stepped into that space of being the household head, they actually began sharing more—they both worked, they both cleaned, they made dinner together. Their marriage looked more "fifty–fifty" than the relationships of many couples who claimed to be egalitarian. As Jennifer Johnson, who emphasized being a submissive wife, ultimately said, "We are going back and forth, and somehow we end up coming together and making [decisions] together."

Like those who wanted to be traditional, couples who wanted to be egalitarian also struggled to implement their values. Workplace policies and social expectations still assume women are responsible for housework and child care. A few couples with egalitarian ideals appeared to enact egalitarian relationships, especially among American-born blacks, but among most couples who said they were egalitarian, men felt their jobs were more important than their wives' jobs, even if the wife made more money. Men also had more free time to go out with friends, play video games, or just do as they pleased. Women both worked and took most of the responsibility for housework and childrearing. While wives of all backgrounds appreciated their husbands' belief in being equal, they were frustrated that equality didn't actually happen.

The balance of power in couples' relationships was entangled with their roles as both workers and parents. While it is normal—even expected—for wives to work for pay in the twenty-first century, norms of gender equality often dissolve when children are added to the mix. It is impossible to look at notions of egalitarianism among married couples with children without distinctly looking at their roles as parents and all of the personal, cultural, social, and structural issues that come with being a mother or a father, as we will explore further in the next chapter.

Notes

1   Durkheim, Émile. 2014. *The Division of Labor in Society.* Edited and with a new introduction by Steven Lukes; translation by W. D. Halls. New York: Free Press.
2   Kingsbury, Nancy, and John Scanzoni. 1993. "Structural-Functionalism." Pp. 195–217 in *Sourcebook of Family Theories and Methods: A Contextual Approach*, edited by P. Boss, W. J. Doherty, R. LaRossa, W. R. Schumm, and S. K. Steinmetz. New York: Plenum Press.
3   Becker, Gary S. 1973. "A Theory of Marriage: Part I." *Journal of Political Economy* 81(4):812–846.
4   Coontz, Stephanie. 2011. *A Strange Stirring: The Feminine Mystique and American Women at the Dawn of the 1960s.* New York: Basic Books.
5   Taylor, Ronald L. 2002. *Minority Families in the United States: A Multicultural Perspective*, 3rd ed. London: Pearson Publishing.
6   Moynihan, Daniel Patrick. 1965. "The Negro Family: The Case for National Action." Washington, D.C.: Office of Policy Planning and Research, United States Department of Labor. Retrieved September 3, 2017 (http://www.dol.gov/oasam/programs/history/

webid-meynihan.htm); Hymowitz, Kay S. 2007. *Marriage and Caste in America: Separate and Unequal families in a Post-Marital Age*. Chicago, IL: Ivan R. Dee, Inc.

7   Collins, Patricia H. 2000. *Black Feminist Thought: Knowledge, Consciousness, and the Politics of Empowerment*. New York: Routledge.

8   Bianchi, Suzanne M., and Melissa A. Milkie. 2010. "Work and Family Research in the First Decade of the 21st Century." *Journal of Marriage and Family* 72(3):705–725.

9   Gerson, Kathleen. 2011. *The Unfinished Revolution: How a New Generation is Reshaping Family, Work, and Gender in America*. New York: Oxford University Press; Pedulla, David S., and Sarah Thébaud. 2015. "Can We Finish the Revolution? Gender, Work–Family Ideals, and Institutional Constraint." *American Sociological Review* 80(1):116–139.

10   England, Paula. 2010. "The Gender Revolution." *Gender & Society* 24(2):149–166.

11   Hochschild, Arlie Russell, and Anne Machung. 2003. *The Second Shift*. New York: Penguin Books.

12   Beere, Carolea, Daniel W. King, Donald B. Beere, and Lynda A. King. 1984. "The Sex-Role Egalitarianism Scale: A Measure of Attitudes Toward Equality Between the Sexes." *Sex Roles* 10:563–576.

13   Wax, Amy L. 1998. "Bargaining in the Shadow of the Market: Is There a Future for Egalitarian Marriage?" *Virginia Law Review* 84:509–672.

14   Schwartz, Pepper. 1995. *Love Between Equals: How Peer Marriage Really Works*. New York: Free Press.

15   Lee, Yun-Suk, and Linda J. Waite. 2005. "Husbands' and Wives' Time Spent on Housework: A Comparison of Measures." *Journal of Marriage and Family* 67:328–336.

16   Harris, Scott R. 2006. *The Meanings of Marital Equality*. Albany NY: State University of New York Press.

17   Allen, Sarah M., and Alan J. Hawkins. 1999. "Maternal Gatekeeping: Mothers' Beliefs and Behaviors That Inhibit Greater Father Involvement in Family Work." *Journal of Marriage and the Family* 61:199–212.

18   Schwartz, 1995.

19   Hill, Shirley A. 2012. *Families: A Social Class Perspective*. Los Angeles, CA: Sage.

20   Glauber, Rebecca, and Kristi L. Gozjolko. 2011. "Do Traditional Fathers Always Work More? Gender Ideology, Race, and Parenthood." *Journal of Marriage and Family* 73:1133–1148.

21   Glauber and Gozjolko, 2011.

22   Allen, William D., and David H. Olson. 2001. "Five Types of African-American Marriages." *Journal of Marital and Family Therapy* 27(3):301–314.

23   Hao, Lingxin. 2007. *Color Lines and Country Lines: Race, Immigration and Wealth Stratification in America*. New York: Russell Sage.

24   Kent, Mary M. 2007. Immigration and America's Black Population. *Population Bulletin* 64(4): 3–16. Retrieved September 12, 2017 (http://www.prb.org/pdf07/62.4immigration.pdf).

25   Momsen, Janet. 1994. *Women and Change in the Caribbean*. London: James Curry.

26   Roopnarine, Jaipaul L. 2013. "Fathers in Caribbean Cultural Communities." Pp. 203–227 in *Fathers in Cultural Context*, edited by David W. Shwalb, Barbara J. Shwalb, and Michael E. Lamb. New York: Routledge.

27   Anderson, Patricia, and Camille Daley. 2015. "African-Caribbean Fathers: The Conflict Between Masculinity and Fathering." Pp. 13–38 in *Fathers Across Cultures: The Importance, Roles, and Diverse Practices of Dads*, edited by Jaipaul L. Roopnarine. Santa Barbara, CA: ABC-CLIO.

28   McAdoo, Harriette P., Sinead Younge, and Solomon Getahun. 2007. "Marriage and Family Socialization among Black Americans and Caribbean and African Immigrants." Pp. 93–116 in *The Other African Americans: Contemporary African and Caribbean Immigrants*

in the United States, edited by Yoku Shaw-Taylor and Steven A. Tuch. Lanham, MD: Rowan and Littlefield.

29   Sudarkasa, Niara. 2004. "Conceptions of Motherhood in Nuclear and Extended Families, with Special Reference to Comparative Studies Involving African Societies." *JENdA: A Journal of Culture and African Women Studies* 5. Retrieved July 15, 2016 (http://www. africaknowledgeproject.org/index.php/jenda/article/view/94).

30   McAdoo et al., 2007.

31   Mwoma, Teresa B. 2015. "Fathering in Kenya." Pp. 410–428 in *Fathers Across Cultures: The Importance, Roles, and Diverse Practices of Dads*, edited by Jaipaul L. Roopnarine. Santa Barbara, CA: ABC-CLIO.

32   Wadende, Pamela A., Kathleen Fite, and Jon Lasser. 2014. "The Kenyan Parent in Changing Times." Pp. 267–276 in *Parenting Across Cultures: Childrearing, Motherhood and Fatherhood in non-Western Cultures*, edited by Helaine Selin. New York: Springer.

33   United States Department of Labor. 2017. *Women in the Labor Force*. Retrieved September 12, 2017 (https://www.dol.gov/wb/stats/stats_data.htm).

5

CONTEMPORARY BLACK
MARRIAGE AND PARENTING

Mia Davis, a working-class Caribbean wife, opens the door to the tiny apartment she shares with her husband, James, also Caribbean, and their two preschool-aged daughters. The girls run in to say hello, the younger one clutching a white doll. Mia settles on the green couch in the cramped but tidy living room, and the girls snuggle against her. James joins us, sitting in an easy chair opposite from Mia and the girls. Mia helps 2-year-old Anna wrap her doll in a towel as 4-year-old Kara pretends to feed hers with a plastic bottle. The girls chatter about their plans for a tea party. James turns to them and says, "You need to be quiet now. Go play in your room." The girls retreat silently.

As we all know too well, stories about single mothers, deadbeat dads, and children who drop out of school and get caught up in gang activity dominate media representations of African-American families. Mothers, in particular, are pilloried for having children outside of marriage, for not offering enough supervision, and for not being good enough role models. Married black couples and black middle-class families are rarely in these narratives. While it is true that the majority of black children in the United States are born to unmarried couples, many are not, and some couples who are not married at the time of their child's birth do eventually marry. More than a third of black children, like Anna and Kara Davis, live with two married parents. Poverty rates among blacks have declined, from over 40% in 1966 to 27% in 2012,[1] and married couples have seen the strongest income gains.[2]

Marriage and Childbearing

This is a book about marriage, but nearly all of the study couples we interviewed had children together, many—but not all—before they officially tied the knot. Regardless of when the children arrived, couples felt having children changed the nature and purpose of their relationships. As Taylor McCoy, a working-class Caribbean wife, said, "The children, they're the fruits of [marriage], and they're the reward, they're the labor … I do believe marriage without kids, it's totally—I think it will be a whole different thing." Overall, these couples had a variety of opinions about when to get married, when to have children, and the relationship between marriage and parenting. In their study of low-income mothers in Philadelphia, Kathryn Edin and Maria Kefalas found that many wished to become more financially stable and to test the dedication and responsibility of their children's father before committing to marriage.[3] Many of our couples who waited to marry until after parenting together for several years told us similar stories.

Some working-class and lower-income fathers experienced a stronger urge to marry if there was a son involved. Gwen Byrd, a working-class, American-born black mother with two biological children and two stepdaughters, was surprised when her husband indicated that their son's birth had influenced his plans to marry her: "Is that part of the reason you married me? Because I gave you your first son?" Her husband nodded, "Uh huh." The interest in parenting sons was expressed across couples of all backgrounds. Ted Posner, a white father of three who did not finish high school and works in a warehouse, said he pressured his wife to marry after their second child, a son, was born: "[W]ell, I had my boy then."

College-educated couples were more likely to marry directly in response to a pregnancy. For Dixon Ryan, originally from the Caribbean, his wife's pregnancy "sealed the coffin" on marriage so that their child would have "an actual family" and not "just a mommy and daddy." Other couples had already planned to marry before they discovered they were expecting. Only Amy Abbas, a white mother with a master's degree, described her decision to marry as a response to embarrassment: "I guess it's best to be honest. We became pregnant." No black couple, regardless of class or country of origin, described out-of-wedlock pregnancy as embarrassing, whether for themselves or others.

For couples who married before having children, becoming parents often seemed like the next logical step in life, and pregnancy was usually planned. Charlene Kelly, a working-class, American-born black mother, was pleased with her decision to have a child with her new husband: "[E]verything was coming together ... I wanted to complete my circle." For middle-class black couples, marriage before childbearing could be a source of pride. After explaining that there was never a perfect time to have children, Lamar Albright, a Caribbean father, said that after five years of marriage, he and his wife deserved to become parents: "Why punish ourselves? We did everything right." Though their children were loved and wanted, middle-class white couples often seemed to see having children as an obligation of marriage. As Allen Kennedy, a white father of three, told us that once he married, "There was no reason not to [have kids]. Once you get married, it's, 'Might as well have some kids.'"

Good Parents ... and Bad Ones

Americans often look for a "right way" to parent, though rarely is there broad consensus about what that way might be. By determining a best way to parent, those who follow this "right" path can increase their own confidence by pointing to other parents who are doing it all wrong. Any trouble with children, even poor report cards or playground scuffles, can be blamed on "bad" parents. Lower-income black children's difficulties, in particular, are hardly ever attributed to structural racism, low-quality schools, or shoddy housing that leads to lead poisoning and asthma. Instead, many identify the root of black children's problems on their parents who, because of their personal and social deficiencies, are using all the wrong practices with all of the wrong tools.

The couples in our study saw themselves as dedicated parents, and for many, the children became more important than the marriage itself.

Mia Davis had great dissatisfaction with her marriage—her husband betrayed her by not revealing that he already had four children with other women until after they were married. The child support he owed made it impossible for his income to cover his current family's needs, and as explained in the previous chapter, he didn't handle their family budget well. But Mia couldn't imagine working full-time herself when her girls were so young, much less leaving them fatherless. As Taylor McCoy, who like the Davises is Caribbean, told us of her marriage, "It's all about the children." Her husband nodded. Mia seemed to feel the same, and James did too—at least about the children he has with Mia.

A few parents referred to having less time alone or experiencing a loss of independence after having kids, but most couples, especially mothers, seemed to think giving up a childless lifestyle should be expected, even welcomed. Only one couple, the Barlows, American-born black and middle class, said that they wished they weren't parents so that they could have more money, freedom, and time for each other; no other couple said anything about wishing or waiting to be child-free. The few childless couples we interviewed were either planning to have children or experiencing infertility. It was common for couples to say that children were the best thing about being married, and as one African couple noted, that they helped to keep the couple together and brightened "gloomy days."

But are devoted parents always doing parenting right? A cursory search on parenting in the books section of Amazon.com generates well over 100,000 titles. Clearly, if there were a magic formula for raising perfect children, only one book would be necessary. Even if there were a book for each year of childhood, with a few more thrown in for special situations, the titles would number under 100. Are there really 100,000 ways to be a good parent?

Scholars, social workers, psychologists, and others often suggest a universal, normative ideal of parenting based on classifications Diane Baumrind developed in the 1960s.[4] She typified three basic categories: "Authoritative" parenting is generally touted as best, while "authoritarian" and "permissive" parenting are considered problematic.

Authoritarian parents have unbending rules, expect obedience, and use corporal punishment. Permissive parents, on the other hand, try to reason with children rather than exercising overt control. They use praise rather than punishment, but they do not define clear expectations or standards for children's behavior. In Baumrind's classifications, authoritative parents offer the best of both worlds. They are not rigid but instead recognize their children's individual needs and talents. Although they reason with their children, they also set standards and exert control when needed.

Sociologists often embrace Baumrind's classifications, but they add considerations of the vital impacts of social locations such as race and class. In the 1960s, Mel Kohn found that families in which the father had a blue-collar job, such as factory or construction work, tended to practice what Baumrind called authoritarian parenting, with high value placed on obedience to rules. Families in which the father held a white-collar job, such as a doctor or engineer, were more likely to emphasize self-direction, practicing a more permissive or authoritative style. Kohn argued that parenting practices reproduced social class across generations because the social skills children learned would work best in careers similar to those of their fathers.[5]

In her book *Unequal Childhoods*, Annette Lareau added race to Kohn's findings about social class. She found that, regardless of race, middle-class parents practiced "concerted cultivation," providing children with structured activities and teaching them to communicate confidently with adults. Working-class parents practiced "natural growth," allowing their children to socialize independently with extended family networks, providing for their needs without planning out their lives, and teaching them to respect adult authorities.[6] Because middle-class parenting practices appear effective in raising children to become middle class themselves, these practices are often deemed superior to the typical parenting styles found among working-class families. But there is no shortage of criticism for any approach. Recent writings suggest that concerted cultivation has led to "helicopter" parenting:[7] hovering parents are so involved in their children's lives and decisions that the children have difficulty learning to handle adult life on their own. Still more differences arise when we consider parenting practices more broadly. Despite findings of American social research and parents' personal beliefs about how to raise children, anthropological research on families across the globe indicates that there is no universally successful approach, and that worldwide, most children grow to be productive adults regardless of their culture's parenting ideals.[8]

Ideas about typical black families were primarily developed in investigation of American-born blacks, those whose families originally endured forced migration, slavery, Jim Crow, the Great Migration to Northern states, and American social welfare policies. As noted previously, scholars have suggested that black married couples have more egalitarian parenting roles than white couples, perhaps in part because of black mothers' traditionally high employment rates.[9] Because these family practices were seen as different, however, they were also often claimed to be inferior.[10] But black immigration has diversified the contemporary population of American blacks. Nearly 9% of blacks living in the United States in 2015 were foreign-born, compared to about 3% in 1980.[11] Investigations of parenting in the Caribbean and in African countries indicate many different family practices, none of which necessarily align with those of American-born blacks—or whites.

Few black couples in our study said anything specific about working to instill a sense of positive racial identity in their children, but because the focus of our interview was marriage, we didn't ask direct questions about parenting (see Appendix C for interview guide). However, because we interviewed and observed almost all couples in their homes, we were able to take note of art and photos displayed or characteristics of the children's toys. Spontaneous responses on race and childrearing did also arise on occasion. Some black fathers, particularly American-born blacks, pointed to trends of unmarried fatherhood in their communities and noted that they were proud that they had bucked this trend, modeling positive black manhood for their children. African couples sometimes mentioned wanting to instill values from their home countries in their children and choosing to socialize with mostly other African families, trying to avoid assimilating their children to what they saw as inferior American values (though none specifically identified a racial component to these values).

Images we saw in pictures and toys in homes of American-born black families were usually of black family members, angels, movie stars, or dolls. James and Mia's daughter, in contrast, played with a white doll during the interview, something neither parent remarked upon. For Montel and Mercedes Sheldon, a middle-class Caribbean couple, their daughter's racial identity was of greater concern. They specifically noted that she preferred white dolls and told her parents that she herself was white and that she wanted them to be white too. Though Montel found this unnerving, in another part of the interview, he himself expressed prejudice, saying that he was not upset when denied an apartment rental because he was black—instead, he sympathized with the landlord, saying he understood why there might be reluctance to rent to black people in America. Caribbean spouses often expressed surprise at the emphasis Americans in general placed on race. For instance, Kylie Velarde, a black Cuban immigrant whose husband is also Cuban but white, said that black women on the bus frequently commented on her daughter's skin tone and asked about her husband's race, something she couldn't imagine happening in Cuba.

Though African parents were primarily the immigrants who specifically discussed wishing to isolate children from American values by associating mainly with family or others from their home countries, both African and Caribbean families tend to value extended family relationships and having daily interactions with aunts, uncles, cousins, grandparents, and others.[12] In fact, many of our African and Caribbean spouses without relations living in the United States spoke of missing the support of their extended families. At the same time, the literature reports that Caribbean and African fathers often practice what Baumrind would call authoritarian parenting, and families may practice corporal punishment that would be considered overly harsh by American standards.[13] Among the couples we talked with, Caribbeans in particular often mentioned that they felt discipline in their home countries was too harsh, and though they generally spanked their children, they felt they did so much less often and more gently than their own parents had. James Davis, whose family hailed from Jamaica, bitterly recounted the beatings he had suffered at the hands of his father, even after they had immigrated, and though he spanked his own daughters on occasion, he swore he would never do to them what had been done to him.

Although the Caribbean consists of numerous countries geographically separated by water, there is substantial consistency among Caribbean cultures.[14] Generally speaking, marriage and childbearing are frequently separate, with the majority of children born outside of marriage, though their parents may live together and may ultimately marry once their family is well-established.[15] Valued masculine traits such as aggression and competitiveness can conflict with the responsibilities of fatherhood, though men often feel that becoming a father is in itself a display of masculinity.[16] Caribbean men tend to value their financial contributions to their families much more than their involvement in day-to-day childrearing;[17] mothers almost always perform the daily work of raising children and running a household.[18]

Family and parenting practices vary more among the black immigrant couples, especially between families in rural areas and those who live in more westernized cities;[19] however, there are a number of similarities among many African nations as well. Grown children are the social safety net in much of Africa, earning money and supporting elderly parents.[20] Childless marriages are virtually unheard of, and even in areas where women are more likely to be employed, they are primary caregivers for children.[21] Fathers are usually involved only with their older sons.

Mothering and Fathering

Today, there are constant debates about good parenting among most parents, both immigrant and American-born: whether children are better off with a stay-at-home parent, what they should eat, what makes a quality school, how they should learn religion, or how much fathers should participate in childrearing. A study of any Internet parenting board showcases a host of conflicts, mostly among mothers, about these issues and more. Though our interviews focused specifically on marriage rather than parenting, our couples had a lot to say about their roles as parents. When we asked about ideal marriages, parenting roles were always part of the picture. Harold Wilcox, whom we met in Chapter 4, described an ideal marriage as a father working outside the home and the wife staying home to take care of the kids, calling it "the American way." Harold's assessment harkens back to middle-class white ideals of the 1950s, portrayed in sitcoms such as *Leave It to Beaver* or *Father Knows Best*, which presented idealized suburban white families navigating only the most superficial conflicts of daily living, always with charm, humor, and a resolution backed by the benevolent family patriarch. Black couples did not have access to a white picket-fence life in the suburbs in the mid-twentieth century—as we discussed in Chapter 2, housing discrimination often specifically excluded black families from suburban life, while wage discrimination made it challenging for black families to live on one income.

Still, though most were not quite as rigid as Harold Wilcox in their picture of the "American way," most of the black couples we talked with did see providing as a primary, or *the* primary, role of fathers, with involved parenting more of a bonus than an expectation. Even mothers with careers emphasized a father's provider role over their own, and Caribbean husbands and wives—and their white counterparts—were especially likely to emphasize a father's responsibility to provide, as Mia and James Davis did. This was true even when the husband was struggling to provide or was not the household's main provider. Though Mia was the one with a college degree and career ambitions, her work life consisted of babysitting and running a web-based home business on the side, yielding to what she believed was James' role as the household provider. Middle-class Caribbean mother Ava Tompkins out-earned her husband, but she told us: "[The father] should be the head of the household. He should be the provider—but not the sole provider." Similarly, Meredith Kennedy, a middle-class white mother of three who, like Mia, did sales work from home, told us, "The man is responsible for making enough money [while] the wife stays at home with the children." Ethan Springfield, a white, unemployed father whose wife was the sole support of their working-class family, said, "As long as I can put food on the table and clothes on my daughter's back, that's what my main concern is." Despite his intentions, he was unable to contribute any earned income to the family in the past year.

Though they felt men should be providers, as discussed in Chapter 4, some wives, especially American-born black wives, expressed empathy regarding the difficulties black men face in the American workforce. The long trend of wage discrimination that led to American-born black women's historical participation in the workforce cushioned expectations that men must always fill the provider role. Black wives were understanding when their husbands faced unemployment, but they still expected them to be searching for a job.

With Caribbean families such as the Davises, as well as white families, husbands and wives often agreed that the wife should not work, at least not officially, even if the family was in economic distress. For Caribbean families, a wife's work was sometimes seen a threat to the husband's masculinity. As Mia explained as to why she was not working or managing the family's money, "I don't want to take that away from James." For other families, both Caribbean and white, it was important that children not attend daycare. Meredith Kennedy said that kids "have the issues they have" because of daycare. She added, "The bond between children and their parents is important, and if women keep working, they are going to miss out on spending time with their child." Concerns about missed opportunities with children did not extend to fathers. Caribbean and white fathers, including Allen Kennedy, sometimes worked two or even three jobs and had little time at home when their children were awake. Among some Caribbean and white families, daycare was seen as a curse to avoid at all costs. Caribbeans who expressed concerns about daycare generally felt a female family member was the only acceptable care provider other than the mother. James and Mia were so opposed to daycare that when their older daughter was an infant, they left her in the care of a relative in another state until Mia was able to quit her job. During that time, they themselves only saw the baby on weekends. Like Mia and James, Mike and Laura Thompson, a lower-class white couple, felt that financial instability was worth avoiding daycare. Mike said, "I don't want [Laura] to go to work. I don't want the child in daycare," while Laura said, "Daycare is something I'm not interested in. ... How do I give up my kids and give some stranger the pleasure of raising them? I can't bring myself to do it." Trust to care for children did not always extend even to the child's father. Taylor McCoy, a Caribbean mother of four, said she could not possibly work outside the home, even if her husband was available:"Would he be able to stay home with the children and do the things I do? No ... I wouldn't see the end of the week. My girls would probably be hanging by their toes somewhere."

Families from all backgrounds that had more egalitarian values, mothers in the workforce, and children in daycare still saw mothers as primary parents. For mothers, work was supposed to be secondary to parenting, no matter how important the wife's career was to her or how much her income contributed to the family's finances. As Kenneth Buckley, a middle-class African father with a working wife, said of the importance of motherhood over work, "we don't have to get so much caught up in the new millennium, where women are getting equally paid, and cross over to the other side where we actually forget what is the major role of a mother." Emmett and Denise Smith, an American-born, middle-class black couple with two sons in preschool, share the work of the home, but Emmett is in charge of cleaning while Denise does "the bulk of the childcare." Aretha Washington, a middle-class, American-born black mother of two, said, "[S]ometimes I pull most of the weight, especially with the boys ... I would assume 98 percent of the responsibilities with my sons." Pamela and Richard Taylor, a middle-class, white couple with two boys, both do household tasks, and during their interview, both got up at different points to attend to their rambunctious toddler. But even though Richard is an involved father, and Pamela is the family's primary breadwinner, Pamela could not imagine Richard as a primary parent as long as she was available. Flustered, she said, "I don't think he would—he could—take care of them on a full-time basis by himself. ... I guess he could do it if he had to, like if I were to die or something."

Even when the father was unemployed and thus home with his children, he usually did not function as a primary parent. Reggie Morrison, an unemployed Caribbean father in a working-class couple, cares for the couple's young children during the day but expects that his wife will take charge the moment she comes home from work. We interviewed only one couple in which the father assumed the responsibilities of a primary parent. Bart McAllister, an American-born black father, has a son from a previous relationship; his wife Lori, who had an American black father but was raised solely by her white mother, has no biological children. Lori likes Bart's son but does not see herself as a mother. Bart is only sporadically employed and takes full responsibility for nearly all childrearing tasks, but—confirming that even he does not see primary parenting as a father's role—he calls himself "Mr. Mom."

Despite the tangential role expected of many fathers both in the United States and in immigrants' home countries, most fathers in our study, both immigrant and American-born, did value spending time with their children in addition to their role as providers. Barry Adams, a lower-class, American-born black father of four, spoke proudly of coaching his son's baseball team. Kingston Kolfi, a lower-class African immigrant, said, "I should be the provider. Come home, happy to see my family [and] spend time with my family." Isaiah Scott, a working-class father also from Africa, discussed the importance of work–life balance: "I can make more money, but I can't have more than 24 hours. It is important that the children get everything from me in terms of time, warmth, and attention." Mike Thompson, lower class and one of our white husbands who vehemently opposed daycare, said of his upcoming leave from work, "I don't get enough time with the baby, and I am going to take full advantage of this week to be with him." Even though fathers almost universally thought mothers should be primary parents, most still saw fathers as important. As Mohammed Abbas, a middle-class father and immigrant from Central Asia, said, "When your child is 16 years old and someone says, 'tell me about your father' [and the response is] 'I've barely seen him'—it shouldn't be that way."

Sometimes society suggests a father's role should primarily be that of a disciplinarian, making the phrase "wait until your father gets home" into a cliché. A few fathers were their family's primary disciplinarian, even though they were a secondary parent, but almost all families had one parent who was stricter than the other, and that person was often the mother. Both mothers and fathers who were the enforcer in the family complained that the other parent was "too soft," while the more permissive parent complained that the strict parent was too harsh or worried too much about trivial rules. Jennifer Johnson, a middle-class, American-born black wife, doesn't like having to play "bad cop" and gave a recent example:

Because of how tight the evening was, there really wasn't time to squeeze in the batting cage because they ended up coming home late and doing homework that was not done. When Marvin does things like this, the children look at me as the mean one because I will say it isn't a good idea—just trying to use parental judgment—and then they won't want to get up in the morning.

For his part, Marvin (also American-born black) said, "[Our daughter] likes to wear crazy color mixtures and fashions and Jennifer gets in an uproar about it—nothing to stress about to me." Caribbean fathers most often identified discipline as one of their responsibilities, but as was the case with James Davis, several remarked that they liked that Americans did not practice the harsh corporal punishment they themselves experienced as children.

Identity, Structure, and Parenting

Overall, one social identity rarely determined universal values, attitudes, or practices regarding parenting among study couples. American-born blacks, Caribbean immigrants, African immigrants, and whites had few practices that were universal either within or among groups. As sociologist Patricia Hill Collins has argued, identities are interactions of race, class, gender, and more—no category alone is sufficient to explain a person's identity.[22] The same may be said of immigration. Black immigrants had as much in common with whites as with American-born blacks. Education, income level, gender, and other factors played roles as well. It is important to note that while "straight-line" assimilation theories[23] assume marriage to be the last stage of immigrant assimilation, occurring after the first generation, a number of our first-generation Caribbean and African immigrants were married to American-born blacks or whites.

Still, some patterns did emerge based on various identity locations, particularly social class. Our lower-income couples, regardless of race or country of origin, generally had children before they married, and none seemed to find this remarkable. Middle-income couples were far more likely to have had all of their children within marriage. While none of these couples condemned out-of-wedlock childbearing, whites said that for themselves, marriage was expected to come first, as when Allen Kennedy said, "Once you get married, it's, 'Might as well have some kids.'" Middle-income black couples sometimes expressed pride that they had not had children before marrying, as when Lamar Albright bragged that he and his wife were married five years before conceiving: "We did everything right."

Interestingly, antipathy toward daycare was most common among lower-income couples, who were also the most likely to be struggling to make ends meet on the father's income alone. This was particularly true among white and Caribbean families. Some stay-at-home mothers did have part-time work, such as home-based sales or occasional babysitting, but only among lower-income families was there an intense belief that mothers should be home with children to the exclusion of outside employment. American-born black couples across the class spectrum did not embrace this point of view. Among Africans, interest in having a stay-at-home mother was expressed as protecting children from assimilating to American values. Although some African mothers wished to stop working in America, some also expressed displeasure that they would be pressured not to work if they lived in their home countries.

Social structures also had significant impacts on family behavior, regardless of parents' values or practices. For instance, black men who had prison records had particular difficulties with employment. Sociologist Devah Pager found that even without a prison record, a black man's chances of landing a job are similar to those of a white man *with* a prison record.[24] The effects of incarceration on employment were generally discussed among lower-income black families, both American-born and immigrant. James Davis, who had spent a great deal of time in prison before meeting and settling down with Mia, felt his record was one of the main factors preventing him from advancing in his job. Though Mia was deeply resentful of the unexpected child support payments James had to make, she never mentioned being angry with James because his prison record could be stunting his income. As was the case with James, all fathers with records said that having children motivated them to stay on the straight and narrow, and they lamented being targeted by the law as black men and the effect their records had on their ability to provide for their families. Two white husbands in our study had criminal justice encounters, and one had spent time in prison. Unlike black fathers, however, white fathers seemed to view their experiences with the law as personal, not systemic. No white father ever indicated that he thought he was targeted by the criminal justice system because he was white.

Parenting may be a joy, but it is also complicated and hard work, which is why those 100,000 books exist. Despite popular perceptions to the contrary, black families have neither universally shared practices nor a universally shared understanding of what constitutes good parenting. In this, they are no different from white people or any other people around the world. As the experiences of the parents in this chapter show, determining the "right" way to do it depends on a host of factors, including race, socioeconomic status, cultural mores, country of origin, and personal experience. Still, both structure and culture impact black parenting, just as they affect other aspects of black family life. We now turn to a discussion of the structures that impacted our families.

Notes

1   DeSilver, Drew. 2014. "Who's Poor in America? 50 Years into the 'War on Poverty,' a Data Portrait." *Pew Research Center*. Retrieved September 11, 2017 (http://www.pewresearch.org/fact-tank/2014/01/13/whos-poor-in-america-50-years-into-the-war-on-poverty-a-data-portrait/).
2   Fry, Richard, and D.Vera Cohn. 2010. "Women, Men and the New Economics of Marriage." *Pew Research Center's Social & Demographic Trends Project*. Retrieved September 11, 2017 (http://www.pewsocialtrends.org/2010/01/19/women-men-and-the-new-economics-of-marriage/).
3   Edin, Kathryn, and Maria J. Keflas. 2011. *Promises I Can Keep: Why Poor Women Put Motherhood Before Marriage, with a New Preface*. Berkeley: University of California Press.
4   Baumrind, Diana. 1967. "Child Care Practices Anteceding Three Patterns of Preschool Behavior." *Genetic Psychology Monographs* 75:43–88.
5   Kohn, Melvin L. 1977. *Class and Conformity: A Study in Values, with a Reassessment*. Chicago: University of Chicago Press.
6   Lareau, Annette. 2003. *Unequal Childhoods: Class, Race, and Family Life*. Berkeley: University of California Press.
7   Skolnikoff, Jessica, and Robert P. Engvall. 2014. *Young Athletes, Couch Potatoes, and Helicopter Parents: The Productivity of Play*. Lanham: Rowman & Littlefield.
8   Lancy, David F. 2015. *The Anthropology of Childhood: Cherubs, Chattel, Changelings*. Cambridge: Cambridge University Press.
9   McAdoo, Harriette P., Sinead Younge, and Solomon Getahun. 2007. "Marriage and Family Socialization among Black Americans and Caribbean and African Immigrants." Pp. 93–116 in *The Other African Americans: Contemporary African and Caribbean Immigrants in the United States*, edited by Yoku Shaw-Taylor and Steven A. Tuch. Lanham, MD: Rowan and Littlefield.

10 United States Department of Labor, Office of Policy Planning and Research. 1965. *The Negro Family: The Case for National Action*. Retrieved March 3, 2006 (http:/www/dol/gov/oasam/programs/history/webid-moynihan.htm).

11 Anderson, Patricia, and Camille Daley. 2015. "African-Caribbean Fathers: The Conflict Between Masculinity and Fathering." Pp. 13–38 in *Fathers Across Cultures: The Importance, Roles, and Diverse Practices of Dads*, edited by Jaipaul L. Roopnarine. Santa Barbara, CA: ABC-CLIO.

12 McAdoo, Younge, and Getahun, 2007.

13 Anderson and Daley, 2015.

14 Roopnarine, Jaipaul L., and Ziarat Hossain. 2013. "African American and African Caribbean Fathers." Pp. 223–243 in *Handbook of Father Involvement*, edited by Natasha J. Cabrera and Catherine S. Tamis-LeMonda. New York: Routledge.

15 Anderson and Daley, 2015; Roopnarine and Hossain, 2013.

16 Anderson and Daley, 2015.

17 Anderson and Daley, 2015.

18 Roopnarine and Hossain, 2013.

19 Mwoma, Teresa B. 2015. "Fathering in Kenya." Pp. 410–428 in *Fathers Across Cultures: The Importance, Roles, and Diverse Practices of Dads*, edited by Jaipaul L. Roopnarine. Santa Barbara, CA: ABC-CLIO.

20 Nyarko, K. 2014. "Childrearing, Motherhood, and Fatherhood in Ghana." Pp. 231–239 in *Parenting Across Cultures: Childrearing, Motherhood and Fatherhood in non-Western Cultures*, edited by Helain Selin. New York: Springer.

21 Mwoma, 2015.

22 Collins, Patricia H. 2000. *Black Feminist Thought: Knowledge, Consciousness, and the Politics of Empowerment*. New York: Routledge.

23 Gordon, Milton M. 1964. *Assimilation in American Life the Role of Race, Religion and National Origins*. New York: Oxford University Press.

24 Pager, Devah. 2007. *Marked: Race, Crime, and Finding Work in an Era of Mass Incarceration*. Chicago: University of Chicago Press.

6

IS MARRIAGE FOR BLACK PEOPLE?

ETHNIC PERCEPTIONS OF BLACKS AND THE INSTITUTION OF MARRIAGE

Danny and Alena Chebet were raised Catholic in Kenya. Alena said that "Catholic guilt" shaped their outlook on marriage to some degree. She explained that if they were to ever divorce or separate, it would "let their families and culture down." No one in her family has divorced or separated, which led her to believe that "divorce is not an option." By contrast, Alena believed that American-born blacks have a more individualistic view of marriage than the Africans she knew.

Just as we had, Stanford University law professor Ralph Richard Banks read the *Washington Post* article in 2006 reporting on the stunning marital sentiments of a class of black sixth-grade schoolchildren. As Joy Jones reported,

> "Marriage is for white people." That's what one of my students told me some years back when I taught a career exploration class for sixth-graders at an elementary school in Southeast Washington. I was pleasantly surprised when the boys in the class stated that being a good father was a very important goal to them, more meaningful than making money or having a fancy title. "That's wonderful!" I told my class. "I think I'll invite some couples in to talk about being married and rearing children." "Oh, no," objected

one student. "We're not interested in the part about marriage. Only about how to be good fathers." And that's when the other boy chimed in, speaking as if the words left a nasty taste in his mouth: "Marriage is for white people."[1]

Banks was so impacted by the children's comments that he chose *Is Marriage for White People?*[2] as the title of his controversial 2011 book. As Banks explains,

> I embraced [the young child's] observation as a title though because it confronted directly the sort of unpleasant reality that adults often seek to avoid. I transformed his statement into a question to match the sense of exploration and curiosity that pervades the book.[3]

He ultimately argues that the contemporary black marriage "problem" lies in black women's narrow thinking about interracial marriage. McDonald wrote a detailed review of Banks' book expressing deep concern for Banks' lack of sensitivity to black women's strong loyalty to black men as husbands.[4] But she also praises Banks for performing—as have numerous others preceding him[5]—a rich literature and statistical review of the socio-structural phenomena that have historically and contemporarily undermined the black population's marital stability.

Such phenomena are deeply reflective of American society as a whole. Like every other society, America is sustained by a number of interdependent social institutions. These institutions exist to help order and structure the lives of its people, to provide them vital resources and services, and to foster social unity. This is achieved by establishing institutional norms and practices to which people conform in varying degrees. Among these enduring and overlapping institutions are our political, legal, educational, business and labor, and cultural (including religious and media) systems. Despite the good intentions these institutions may have, each is highly racialized and gendered so as to affect ethnic black, white, Hispanic, Asian, and other Americans in distinguishable and significant ways.

The family is also one of these social institutions, existing primarily to support intimate interpersonal relationships, protect the welfare of children, ensure human reproduction, and assimilate its citizens to all of the other social institutions. While there has been much debate about what is considered to be a legitimate family form—such as the debate over female-headed families and over the recognition of families led by same-sex couples—it is the general consensus that the family is the bedrock of society and marriage the bedrock of the family. Nonetheless, the institution of marriage (like all other institutions) is elastic and ever-evolving, and as a result the experience and perception of marriage differ in a number of ways across ethnic lines. A central objective of this text is to highlight that this variation is true even *among* African Americans.

All of these social institutions, in combinations of intentional and unintentional ways, produce and reinforce ethnic and gender inequalities. Even as "[l]aws against discrimination, changing gender norms, migration, and economic necessity have all resulted in notable advances by women and racial/ethnic minorities" (124),[6] sharp social inequalities persist. African-American marriages are affected by institutionalized sexism, racism, and classism,[7] while the everyday practices of social institutions—guided by social attitudes and ideologies of the dominant culture—result in greater socioeconomic hardship and distorted images of black marriage.

As we have noted throughout, our work is motivated largely by the fact that black intimate relationships have been judged against the traditional, normative bounds of the institution of *the family* (see Chapter 1). Numerous scholars have criticized this judgment as harsh and ethnocentric. There has been a heavy preoccupation with the disparate demographic trends in divorce and non-marriage between black and white Americans in marriage research and less attention to donning a proper socio-historical lens to fully interpret them. As a result, we now find people questioning whether marriage in America is in large measure incompatible with black people.

Thus, we thought it important to gather reactions from our study couples to the "marriage is only for white people" sentiment. We did so by introducing the couples to the passage from Joy Jones' *Washington Post* article (see above) during the course of the research interview. Our analysis of these responses, combined with those from our exchanges with the couples about their marital ideologies (i.e. what they saw as the "ideal" marriage), reveals that ethnic variation exists around the contentious subject of African-American commitment (or lack thereof) to the institution of marriage, and of couples' perceptions of the socio-structural (i.e. institutional) factors that shape black marital experience. While most couples espoused basic ideas like good mate selection and "true love," friendship, cooperation and reciprocity, stick-to-itiveness, and egalitarianism—i.e. their perceptions of "ideal marriage"—responses on socio-structural matters were also front and center. As expected, a central emergent socio-structural theme pertains to the institution and social environment of marriage and the family. But labor and economics, the media, and religion are also addressed. The issues of criminal justice, education, and racism—like all of these subjects—were intertwined. And yet, our black couples did not believe that marriage was not for them. As Tiffany Glasser, a working-class, American-born black wife, said,

> I don't understand why [one would think that marriage is for white people], I really don't ... for me, it's the complete opposite. And that's why I always said I knew I was going to get married. I was surrounded by married people, I always knew that. And that's why to me that's an odd statement

Is the Institution of Marriage for Black People?

Whether husbands and wives across our study sample responded to the "marriage is for white people" claim with astonishment or with some level of agreement, virtually all did believe that this perception is pervasive in America—blatantly and covertly, and not just among African-American children. Most also believe that this claim is born from a lack of exposure to black relationships where marriage actually exists and where divorce does not occur in short order. This lack of exposure is indicative of what many simply call "the environment." And what they generally meant by environment is one or more contexts in which distorted realities of African-American marriage are rooted.

First, it is important to note that a good number of couples across the ethnic groups *simply thought this claim was inaccurate.* They stated that the institution of marriage is obviously alive and well among African Americans either because they themselves are black and married or because they know plenty of other blacks who are. In many cases, they also pointed to their own parents being married for decades and to other black, married couples they encountered regularly in their daily lives. Others emphasized that marriage is certainly available and possible for both black and white people. The McAllisters, lower-class, American-born blacks, were one such couple; they answered, "marriage is for everyone." Allen Kennedy, a middle-class white husband, responded similarly and explained that growing up where he did, marriage was well-represented among all those he knew, white and otherwise. David Russell, a lower-class, American-born black husband, though coming from a very different context, made a similar observation:

> I'm sitting here listening to you [interviewer reading from Joy Jones' article] feeling like that's just kind of an ignorant statement. … I grew up in a [black] project area and there were a lot of people who weren't married, just baby mama, baby father living together. They weren't married. But there were a lot of people that were. There were ladies in their 50s to their 40s to their 30s that were married, who we saw and respected.

David went on to say that many black marriages go unnoticed because they occur without the fanfare of a big wedding due to the fact that many black parents cannot afford to help pay for it: "Most black people's parents say, 'Shit, you'd better help *us*!'"

William Brown, who is working class and white, said that only a "racist" would believe this claim because clearly people of all races, ethnicities, and backgrounds get married. He thought maybe people who say such things are only imagining the case of impoverishment where marriage is more of a "luxury." Brianna Bishop, a working-class, American-born black married to a Ghanaian, argued for a different claim from her perspective: "*Divorce* is for white people!"—a perspective also voiced by some other American-born black and Caribbean participants. Other couples said the bottom line is that marriage is for anyone and everyone who really wants it, black or white, whether one wants to legalize the relationship or not.

That said, the most common response we received to this "white people" claim was that the notion comes from being raised in families and neighborhoods where non-marriage and divorce are prevalent. Almost 60% of such comments were offered by American-born black spouses. Here is a sampling of very similar remarks that were given:

> That's how we were raised thinking. You might not hear it, but you definitely *see that white people are married.*

> [African Americans are] raised and they don't know anything about marriage.

> [The school boy from the news article] hasn't been around a successful marriage his whole life. Just speaking from what he had witnessed.

> Society makes it feel like marriage is for white people. If he's never seen black people married and in a good relationship, then he'd probably be thinking there are none out there. If you've got the idea being bred in your head, you will not [get married]. You cannot keep a marriage. Then that's the way it's going to be. You know, if you believe in that, then that's who you are.

> So if you grew up without a marriage between your parents to speak of, there tends to be an erosion of second, third generation. In no time, no one is getting married.

Several responses given by the white and the immigrant African and Caribbean spouses were in a similar vein. But virtually every immigrant spouse who commented on this matter did so in an explicitly comparative manner. That is, immigrants viewed the "marriage is for white people" notion as uniquely affecting American-born blacks, where American-born blacks seemed to paint a broad stroke.

In discussing this issue, immigrants mainly focused on cultural differences and specific demographic trends that more often than not favored the immigrant experience over the experience of the American-born. Tracey Buckley, middle class and originally from Sudan, raised a point she thought was of particular importance:

> Well, I can tell you in my 31 years of life, I do not know of
> anybody who was born out of wedlock in Sudan. ... As for me,
> I didn't know you could have children without being married
> until I was [in my teens]. I never thought of that before. So, to
> answer your question about [marriage is for white people], I
> don't think it is.

She went on to say that, to her knowledge, out-of-wedlock childbearing
is also uncommon among Hondurans (we are not sure what her experience with Hondurans has been). Kenyan spouses talked about how their
culture also made things like divorce unthinkable. Alena Chebet said that
divorce or separation would make her feel as if she were failing her family and culture, but she noted that American-born blacks don't seem to
have that burden. She said that they adopt a more "individualistic" view
of marriage. All of this was generally cast as American-born couples lacking "moral discipline."

The theme of American-born blacks' individualism was a central current. Many of these couples feel that American-born blacks have lost
sight of the idea that marriage is as at least as much about being embedded in extended family and community as it is about the spousal relationship:[8] "I think this individualistic attitude is counterproductive," was how
Hannah Dawit, a middle-class, American-born black woman married
to an Ethiopian, succinctly put it. Some believed that this individualism
also created unhealthy competition between spouses, particularly when
it involved money. Samantha Trotter, who is Guyanese, put it this way:

> [T]hey try and be in marriages but still hold onto a lot of, you
> know, "what's mine is mine, and what's yours is yours." Try to keep
> that individuality. When you come of here [to America], you pool
> your resources for kind of the bigger good type of thing. And that's
> not something I observed when I came here, you know, with black-
> American families.

To a lesser degree, these couples isolated father absenteeism (and to an
even lesser degree, single motherhood) in contributing to the image of
black marriages as unstable. Morgan Peterson (Jamaican) said she feels
that the experience of American-born blacks is very different from that

of either whites or Jamaicans because of frequent father absence. Her husband, Landon, followed by contradicting Morgan somewhat in saying that black men in the United States don't support their children as much as white men, but that in Jamaica fathers don't support their children as well as those in the United States emotionally and financially. Kalinda Goodman, a middle-class Kenyan wife, spoke much like Morgan but was more expressive:

> The men are not ready to take care of their kids. They just get someone pregnant and when [it's time to take care of the baby], they're not there. I don't know the reason why, but I know that most men—black American men—they don't take responsibility for their families.

The issue of infidelity among American-born men was raised by a few African couples and described as projecting from their need to demonstrate male "power" and contributing to this father absenteeism (infidelity will be discussed further in Chapter 7). Like Morgan above, a number of the Caribbeans indicated they felt that the need to exert masculinity seemed to result in infidelity, divorce, and informal polygamy more frequently among their population of immigrants than among the American-born, collectively undermining father–child engagement.

Even as many of the black immigrant couples argued that American-born couples are more egalitarian than both immigrant blacks and white couples (see Chapter 4)—even showing admiration[9]—they worried that perhaps too much freedom and power has been afforded these wives and that this might help explain the ethnically disparate marriage statistics. What they referenced primarily here was the ever-increasing number of these wives advancing socioeconomically beyond their husbands.[10] Travon Sesay, working class and from Cameroon, asserted, "I think because in too many [American-born] marriages, most of the time women make more money than the husband. It can be a problem for the marriage sometimes." Many said that this problem is equally prevalent among American-born blacks even during the dating stage of the relationship. Ryan Trotter, who is American-born, asserted (as did his wife

Samantha) that obtaining higher degrees is becoming more common among American-born black women, making it more difficult for them to find a partner of equal stature. When they do manage to marry, he said, they often still want "old school men" despite the non-traditional gender arrangement and tension (even divorce) that percolates from men feeling inferior: "There are a limited number of [equally successful] black men; everyone's chasing the same few."

We hesitated in presenting what was one of the most disturbing discussions we had on the "white people" claim. But we ultimately thought it was worth including, given the ongoing struggle for the protection of women around the globe. Kalinda Goodman stated that she saw immigrant blacks going the (wrong) way of the American-born with their marriages. She focused on how immigrant blacks come to America and get exposed to things that are disruptive to marriage, that upset the gender *balance*, and that lead to divorce. Best we clarify why we were so disturbed by simply presenting Kalinda's own words:

> I think [black immigrant] women take advantage. Like you know, back home there are husbands who beat their wife. But when they come here, a man has no right to beat up a wife or something. But that woman takes advantage to where when that man tries to beat her up, she calls 9-1-1 and the man will be taken off. So, they take advantage until this man is so fed up with this woman calling 9-1-1 for the cops to come and get him, so the man is like, you know, I don't need you. ... So I find that they take advantage of their rights here, and they just do whatever they do and the man is fed up or the woman is fed up and they just break up.

This was not a common sentiment among immigrant couples by any means. Other immigrant women mentioned that domestic abuse is common and accepted in their home countries, though they themselves did not think that it was acceptable. Our raising this issue here helps us to remember how cultural ideas and practices within the African diaspora vary dramatically against the backdrop of different levels of protection and regard for human rights.

The Media

In the previous section, we learned that the study couples are quite cognizant that the "marriage is for white people" claim springs primarily from a lack of exposure to the many black marital relationships that exist. They convey that the images of black relationships that most Americans are exposed to are overly laden with issues of out-of-wedlock childbearing, divorce, individualism versus spousal and community partnership, father absenteeism, male infidelity, and greater socioeconomic advancement by wives than husbands. The couples describe these images, cemented in our minds, as funneling through the narrow scope of hyper-segregated neighborhoods, schools, families, and other social spaces.

In this section, we focus on yet another element of the distortion of black marriage that pervades society at large and that virtually all of the study couples noted as highly significant to this distortion: the institution of mass media. Marci Bounds Littlefield, in her work on "media as a system of racialization,"[11] states in solid terms what you will see our study couples saying in their own way:

> Although many vehicles inform the hegemonic social structure, the media are the primary agent of socialization in which participants are seduced, educated, and transformed by ideas concerning race, gender, and class on a global level, and these ideas often support White supremacist capitalist patriarchy. (676)

In staying in line with the basic terminology of this chapter, hegemonic social *institutions* are those that structure their everyday actions in accordance with the ideas held by those in power. America is often interpreted as a hegemonic entity, whereby all of its institutions are governed by the prevailing thought of those who possess the strongest political and economic power. Littlefield goes on to say that these power brokers—overwhelmingly white, elite men—are well known to "[support] images that degrade minorities" to garner endorsement of their ideas and/or to make a profit, such as with popular music and videos. Thus, Littlefield attests to how our mass media "educates" the public about black people through the prism of these power brokers, where black people are regularly and vigorously cast as inferior social beings (for some, blacks are even thought of as inferior *biological* beings). When black people buy into the negative portrayals that are promoted by the media, they are said to be experiencing internalized racism; that is, they sometimes come to accept the images and ideas they are bombarded with as truth. We kept our eyes open for such incidents but found few obvious signs of this problem among our black married couples. On the other hand, we did find that black couples were very confident that the media play a significant role in shaping the claim that marriage is for white people.

Of the various forms of media that we access every day, television was by far the source that study couples mentioned most often as promoting stereotypes of black marriage. Movies were also mentioned, as were popular black magazines. All were blamed for portraying black women as desperate or uninterested in marriage. In some cases, any one and all of these sources were simply referred to as "the media," which might in the minds of these couples have included other mediums such as newspapers, advertising, sports, social media, or video games. One couple did make a statement about "commercials" and their neglect of black marriage imagery, and another about hip-hop artists and athletes serving as more prominent role models than stable, black married couples. It matters how often blacks see themselves positively represented, "as it contributes to perceptions of group vitality and standing in society" among their own and other groups (4).[12]

American-born blacks were again the group providing the largest share of comments. The immigrants had less to say, and the white contribution came only from one couple. The majority of the American-born couples believed television to be the primary media culprit in circulating stereotypes[13] about black relationships in both the black and white communities. There were many echoes of, "All you see on TV is white married people" and, "You just don't see black married people on TV." With such high television consumption in many homes, some blacks felt that black relationship images managed to make the viewer—especially the child viewer—believe that *all* black households must be like his or her single-headed household and that marriage is simply not part of the culture. Jennifer and Marvin Johnson, a middle-class, American-born black couple, also included the media's oversimplification of black male incarceration as something that sorely exacerbated some black children's real experience with the subject. In his comments on this subject, Emmett Smith, a middle-class, American-born black husband, drifted back to those sixth-grade schoolchildren Joy Jones wrote about in the *Washington Post*:

> [They] watch a lot of TV and, unfortunately, African Americans are categorized unfortunately as broken homes and drug-infested, and in that nature. He may even live in that situation. So he hasn't been exposed to a positive African-American marriage. You only speak that which you know about. ... So that's what [they were] thinking: All you see on TV is the perfect white family.

Netra Gardner, a working-class, American-born black wife, shared Emmett's sentiment but optimistically said that "on TV, in different places, in the malls ... you see [happily married black couples] a lot more now."

Black immigrant couples joined in the chorus. Among them were the Addys, a middle-class African couple, who were really the only ones among the Africans to speak directly to the media and its black marriage representation. Alexis Addy used the term "misrepresentation" to describe what has caused damage to black people and their reputations as marital partners. She was hopeful, though, that the warm embrace the public had given Barack and Michelle Obama as a couple would help "reverse" people's way of thinking about what black marriages can be (President Obama was just winding up his first term when the Addys were interviewed). The Caribbean immigrant couples were a bit more represented here. Samantha Trotter noted that black media, such as black women's magazines, makes it seem that black men are completely out of reach as marriageable partners for black women. The Tompkins couple said that media portrays rap, hip-hop, and sports stars as the only viable role models for black men, and that stars are not usually paragons of husbandly responsibility.

Donald Craft, who is from Trinidad, and his wife Sandra, who is American-born black, are a middle-class couple who decided that, instead of noting *the absence* of blacks on television, they would try to recall where they *had* seen representations of black marriage. The interview dialogue went like this (it's worth showing the entire conversation):

Sandra: On television you see the white people. They are married, you know, that is what you see. But on, like, a lot of black shows you see (otherwise). Except for, like of course, not like *The Cosby Show* and stuff like that.

Interviewer: What shows do we have now with black people that are married? Let me think …

Donald: None.

Sandra: Let's see, they … no they are divorced. I am thinking …

Donald: I was going to say *The Practice*. That is one. Is it called *The Practice*?

Sandra: *Grey's Anatomy*, but the one that hmmm … It is called *The Practice* with Taye Diggs. But they are divorced. Still work together, but they are divorced.

Interviewer: There aren't any black prime time shows …

Sandra: There aren't one. Not one.

Interviewer: I have been watching a lot of HDTV lately. Oh my god, my husband hates me. At least you do see black couples on *House Hunters*.

Sandra: Yeah. Oh, I do, I watch it. You watch HDTV? The one when they fix up the houses and stuff?

Donald: Oh yeah. I watch it all the time.

Sandra: But that is cable. [And there you find] re-runs of *The Fresh Prince* on Nickelodeon and re-runs of *Good Times*.

Interviewer: And on network TV there is the *House of Payne* now.

Sandra: Oh yeah. That's true.

Donald: That [show is] just a joke. I mean, that is just a bunch of comedians being funny about [real] lives, and I mean that is not reality to me.

Sandra: But you don't have any … you don't see any positives, you know. Even in the movies you really don't see any.

The Crafts themselves are middle class.

Given that most white couples leaned toward non-structural and more cultural explanations for non-marriage or dysfunctional marriage among blacks, we weren't terribly surprised by the nature of Allen Kennedy's discussion about the media. Allen, who is middle class, relied on the "kernel of truth" hypothesis of stereotypes to make his case. He argued, "Stereotypes are based sometimes on truth. It's sad to think that marriage is for white people, but there's some truth to it." The "kernel of truth" hypothesis was originally put forth by psychologist Gordon Allport back in 1954. It states that some stereotypes are based on a bit of truth, though they are often exaggerations of the truth or overlook that the fact on which they are grounded is no longer sound (35).[14] James Waller, in his book *Face to Face: The Changing State of Racism Across America*, quotes David Ayers to help clarify what this means:

> Someone who stereotypes African-Americans as more likely than European-Americans to bear babies outside of marriage or to be on welfare would be correct. But to presume that most nonmarital births or most welfare clients are African-American is to over-generalize because it just isn't so.[15]

In another example, people who rely on a "kernel of truth" in essence take a proportionate statistic—like the proportion of blacks who marry is far lower than the proportion of whites that do—and dismiss its proportional counterpart (blacks who *do* marry) altogether. Perhaps more importantly is that evoking such a stereotype dissuades those who use and/or adopt it from seeking an understanding of the socio-structural forces that brought that "kernel" to bear.

Meredith Kennedy, who we identified earlier as having grown up in an ethnically diverse area, took a different approach than her husband in their interview, based on the same facts:

> in the neighborhood we used to live in, there were quite a few black families still together, married 20 or 30 years. But because it's not what you see every day portrayed on TV, you think that there aren't people out there like that … Just because it's not in your face doesn't mean it's not there. They just, for some reason, the media and TV, likes to show one side of things all the time. … It's like when you look at the crime in the city, just because you don't nec-essarily hear about where a white person did something to a black person, doesn't mean it doesn't happen, or vice versa. Just because it's not in your face doesn't mean it's not there.

In the interview we conducted with Meredith alone, she gave numerous examples of how she often, as in this case, broke ranks with members of her family in making the conscious choice to view black families differently than the whites she knew. She stated that though the majority of her father's clients were black, he frequently used the "n-word." And she described how her mother made a huge fuss about the Kennedys having moved "to the city." The mother was worried that suddenly black people were in sight: "Why are there black people on the corner?" Meredith replied, "They're waiting for a bus." While Meredith did not explicitly state that the media contributed to her parents' racism, she volunteered these details in the midst of our discussion of the media.

Labor and Economics

Not surprisingly, the socioeconomic standing of American-born black couples, relative to white couples and black immigrant couples, was highlighted in our discussions of marital ideals and of whether marriage is something foreign to black people. Most African and Caribbean couples tended to distinguish their marriages and families from those of American-born blacks *and* whites in these comparative statements. On the other hand, American-born black and white couples made no distinction among black ethnics in comparing white marriages to those of blacks. (This does not mean necessarily that they never make black distinctions in their lives regarding marriage, just that those distinctions were not made in the context of our interviews.)

Most American-born couples conveyed that they are well attuned to racial distinctions in marriage related to employment and other economic matters. In some cases, they showed frustration in the frequency of seeing comparatively resource-rich white marriages. Marvin Johnson, for example, said that his family and friends frequently discuss how they regularly see even *young* (emphasis theirs) white couples and their children doing quite well. Further, he said that poor folk among the white married appear better off than poor folk among those blacks who are married. Such realities were clearly wearing on Bart McAllister:

> [I've] just been trying to get that, you know, that "Brady Brunch," kind of lifestyle, I guess. You know everybody's home, everybody's going to school as far as the kids go. And just a good life, as you say.

Have a picket white fence and all. But I can't seem to get that far, you know. I would really have to hit the lottery or something. Get some real good money or [my wife] hits the lottery or just get a good job. ... And right now just finances, really. That seems to be what makes everybody happy. You know, you got money, you can do what you want to do, you can go places. You can have outings and things like that.

Bart suggested here that obtaining the good married life that so many whites enjoy rests on his ability to earn far more than a livable wage, which itself is elusive.[16] With black men being disproportionately under-employed or with no job at all, realizing family dreams is extremely difficult for many black men.

For many decades now, academics and policymakers have detailed what has occurred to make Black men's attachment to the labor force and decent wages so precarious. In 1993—about midway through this socio-logical discourse—Lynda Dickson[17] was one of many to explain that man-ufacturing jobs and slightly higher-level, white-collar jobs were sharply reduced after World War II once many of these jobs were replaced by new technology. The black working class was particularly vulnerable to job displacement as this technology took hold. In time, the black lower class and "underclass" swelled in size. This is perhaps the most significant factor that has led to the growing socioeconomic disparity between blacks and whites. Further, about forty years after this structural economic change began, statistics showed black women became better able to ride the cur-rent of change in the labor market than their male counterparts. This latter point helps to inform the growing socioeconomic disparity between black husbands and wives, as well as the black marital distress we witness today.

Jacob McAvoy, married to a white middle-class wife, reported that he had not suffered from the racial "discrimination" in the United States labor market that he knew American-born black men had. (He had only emigrated from the Ivory Coast five months prior to our inter-view). Therefore, in his mind, neither had his marriage been consciously impacted by gender dynamics stemming from black male and female labor issues, even though Emily was supporting them. Nonetheless, Jacob seemed to identify, as a black man, with the struggles of the

American-born; he clearly understood how black marriages could be stressful when no good jobs are available for husbands. The Trotters both agreed that the labor and economic issues they saw facing black marriages in the United States did not directly affect their marital relationship. However, they said that they shared the belief that black marriages are very likely to crumble under the weight of such stress.

Black wives' steady progress in the labor market and in educational attainment figures again in certain comments. Those of Brandon Helmy, a working-class, American-born black husband, were right in line with the black-male labor force detachment discourse discussed above, as well as with discussion of the economic role black wives have had to play:

> Many black men back in the day really had to leave [their homes] to make money. They had to go elsewhere and get work or barely go home [from work at all]. The women had to be really strong to take care of their whole families. [And] when the men came back, they still had those strong wills.

Brandon went on to suggest that with the economic necessity for American-born wives to intensify their labor force participation came a change in family headship unanticipated by many black husbands:

> Like, [wives would say] "Whoa, you've been gone for a couple of months, and I know you've been sending home money to take care of your kids, but I've been in control of this situation, and I had a ship to run."

(See more on black marriage "headship" in Chapter 4). Some Caribbean husbands lamented that they were forced to relinquish their custom of male headship and were forced to accept that to survive in the United States black wives *have* to significantly supplement the husbands' income (and in many cases, they bring in most of the income).

Some felt that the independence that black women experience from their socioeconomic mobility weakens the stability of black marriage. Abeni Sesay, an American-born black but married to a man from Cameroon, said this almost verbatim, then followed with this:

I see that a lot of women here who have government jobs, they make X amount of dollars, they make more than their husband, more than their mate. And they feel that their mate has to meet their expectations. If not, she [feels she] would rather be alone.

She then offered familiar and denigrating criticisms of African Americans.[18] Makayla Scott, a working-class African wife, suggested that one of the reasons why some black marriages don't survive is that black women prefer to be on their own rather than deal with the economic challenges faced in black marriage.

A number of whites in our sample also offered familiar and denigrating criticisms of American-born blacks when addressing labor and economic issues. For instance, Harold Wilcox, a working-class white husband, said "black people are in a totally different world than regular people, especially inner-city ones." He went on to blame welfare for a lack of marriage among low-income black people, said that all inner-city men who father children are drug dealers and that women having multiple children is "a tax rebate thing for them." Some felt that black couples are uselessly languishing in racial self-pity and using institutional barriers as an excuse for their lack of mobility, particularly given the recent supposed "post-racial" shift. They suggested that socio-structural explanations for black socioeconomic instability were weak. But in doing so, they also described phenomena that actually *support* such explanations, such as when Harold indicated that black people are not considered "regular people" or that blacks are concentrated in inner cities, which was—and still is—a result of housing discrimination that has prevented blacks from purchasing houses in areas occupied by whites. The only other group contributing similar thoughts here—and the contribution was minuscule by comparison—were Caribbean spouses.

The idea of a post-racial society has been circulating since the 1960s, but it became a more broadly popular notion after Barack Obama was elected president in 2008. Bettina Love and colleagues[19] state that post-racial "signifies a society in which racial differences are no longer significant" (3).[20] While post-racialism is thought to be a myth among many scholars, politicians, and everyday folks,[21] plenty of other people strongly believe that we have reached a point in time where "race" does not significantly determine socioeconomic life chances. Yet, much of this interview content on labor and economics supports the idea that racial distinctions among married couples do in fact exist.

Richard and Pamela Taylor, a white middle-class couple, were particularly vocal in their allusions to the post-racial era. Richard was resentful that the only way he could get a college scholarship was to attend a "minority school":

> They [blacks] can get minority scholarships anywhere. I don't understand why that has to be a white or black thing. Why can't it just be based on your merit or who you are ... It's hard to be a white middle-class male than it is for anybody else ... Instead of teaching their kids the negatives of society, teach them or try to put in their heads some of the more positive things that you could do. You know. Because, basically, most of the [black] people I've talked to, it's like, "Why should I even try?"

Here, Richard espoused what has come to be called "white backlash" or "whitelash,"[22] where black mobility is believed to be "engineered" (271)[23] by an ultra-liberal society at the expense of whites. Pamela also gave voice to this idea:

> I hate to say this, but black culture needs to get past that. The need to say, "We can do better." Nobody's holding anybody back anymore. Maybe in the 50s and 60s and 70s. But now I think everybody has the same opportunity of getting out of school as anybody else. And as far as getting married ... why is it just for white people? (271)

Further, Pamela found it "ridiculous" that in black culture there is the notion that women not marrying will "get [them] something more." By this she meant the idea that single black women would rather receive welfare benefits—"free school" and "food stamps"—than to better financially support their children through marriage (Pamela and Richard's son attends "free" public school). And Richard said that the black men he encounters in prison (he is a correctional officer) feel that there is "nothing out there" for them, "so why bother" to reach for better. Other white couples were not so forward, but they dropped a comment here and there with similar sentiment. But like the Taylors, these white couples were unaware that as they put forth their racial criticisms, they also intimated that there *are* institutional barriers to black family mobility, i.e. the welfare system, the criminal justice system, and a poorly performing educational system.

Religion

Lastly, religion was a highly important factor among our study couples. Our analysis of these data was informed by what Anthony Giddens et. al (2009)[24] organize as the three key elements that define religion from the sociological perspective:

1. Religion is a form of *culture*, which consists of the shared beliefs, values, norms, and material conditions that create a common identity among a group of people. Religion has all these characteristics.
2. Religion involves beliefs that take the form of ritualized practices— special activities in which believers take part and that identify them as members of the religious community.
3. Religion provides a feeling that life is ultimately meaningful. It does so by explaining coherently and compellingly what transcends or overshadows everyday life, in ways that other aspects of culture (such as educational system or a belief in democracy) cannot.[25] (528)

In sum, the institutionalization of religion is accomplished through the establishment of formal, structured systems of worship and faith teaching.

Each ethnic study group contributed to this religious content in good measure. But the white couples weighed in far less than black couples on the primary assertion: that the couple highly values religion and that religion plays a central role in their marital lives. There were several couples who expressed that religion was foundational to marriage and vital to marital longevity. These comments were based either on personal experience or on the dictates of their faith. A number of couples, like the American-born Kellys and Crawfords, reported that their churches offered valuable support in defusing various sorts of marital conflict and in developing coping skills. The Dawits (Ethiopian and American-born) said that there was one time when they credited their church and their faith for having saved their marriage. Meredith Kennedy (white) said that she learned "how you treat each other with respect" based on the religious principles she learned from her religiously devout parents, even though she also expressed concern that her parents themselves were racist.

Other couples look to their religion for clarity on interpreting religious texts where marriage is concerned. This interview content reflects primarily American-born and African immigrant couples' desires to conform to religious rules regarding such things as submission, headship, divorce, and plural marriage. Cameroonian Daniel Naki, who is married to a white woman, indicated that his religion, Islam, compels him to be "the provider" and to insist that his wife and daughter cover their heads; he downplays other aspects of Islam that do not treat men and women equally. The Buckleys, Muslims from Sudan, also take the Quran very seriously in regard to marriage. But in one of most intriguing discussions we had on the role of religion, Kenneth Buckley talked about the flexibility he and his wife are forced to employ in order to accomplish their goals in America versus in Africa:

> My religion says that, you know, the typical house is where the household is, man. He take care of things and the woman is the wife and the mother, and things like that. But that's my religion. If I have to abide exactly by my religion, we would have not been where we are. So, I can't just totally implement it [here in the United States]. And we're not letting religion fight it, and it's not like me and my wife are thinking we're doing anything wrong. Because I am her husband and I'm improving that situation for her to go on and get her career.

For some couples, a life of *spirituality* makes better sense to them than to be limited by the dictates of a religious faith. Gerard Saucier and Katarzyna Skrzypińska (2006)[26] find that tradition-oriented religiousness

(TR) and subjective spirituality (SS) are very different constructs and tend to cluster among people with similar personality types. Taylor McCoy, a working-class Caribbean wife, was particularly vocal about this distinction:

> We're spiritual people. And that's what we teach our children, spirituality. It's just that, with us, because we discussed this a long time before, like, before our daughter was born. It's just like I think people get lost in religion. And I think religion is set up to divide people rather than bring them together. And so I'm not really going to uphold anything that's based on separation of people based on their religious belief. I don't believe that, and I don't think any religion should do that. So we just find ourselves to be more spiritual than religious. Like, we're not going to like praise any denominations, but we're not going to reject it. Because I believe everybody has a path, everyone is going towards the same light, but everybody has a different path. And it's just not to be judgmental towards those that have their separate path.

Yet despite these strong convictions, the McCoys never spoke of any connection between their spiritual ideals and their marital life. Note also that Taylor finds religion divisive, where Saucier and Skrzypińska argue that religion is more associated with collectivism and spirituality more self-focused.

Some couples (or at least one of the spouses) were very outspoken about the need to embrace multiple faiths to meld a strong spiritual life. Lamar Albright (Trinidadian) is described as having delved into a wide range of religious teachings to forge a very individual spirituality. We were told by his wife that it was not unusual for Lamar to at one moment attend a mosque, then at another attend a temple (type not named), a Kingdom Hall (Jehovah's Witness), or a church. Lamar said that he searches for the similarities that exist across faiths and incorporates those similarities into his spiritual existence. Similarly, American-born David and Sharon Russell claimed to embrace the teachings and beliefs of multiple faiths for spiritual enlightenment. But they are quite critical of any religious requirement of submissiveness for wives.[27]

There were a handful of black and white couples who expressed very succinctly that they were *not* religious in any way. For example, the Velardes (Cuban) expressed that even though Fidel Castro claimed Cuba as secular rather than atheist in 1992[28]—loosening restrictions on religious expression—they never felt the need to adopt any religious identity there or in the United States. The Larsons, a white couple, stated, "We're not really religious, so to speak; but we had [our wedding] in a church anyway because we wanted a real wedding." The Martins, a working-class, American-born black couple, reported that while both of them were active in church for much of their lives, they had not participated in anything religious for many years.

Then there were couples who professed to be religious but where one or both spouses engaged in little or no religious activity. No Caribbean immigrants were represented among these particular claims. The Wallers (white) acknowledged that they are bothered that their children had not yet taken their Communion and do not attend Confirmation classes. Michelle works a lot of hours and finds it hard to wake up Sunday mornings. Andrew just hasn't found a place of worship that works for him yet. He tried to go to a Christian (Protestant) church because he knew this would please his wife, but he said he is more comfortable and believes more strongly in Catholicism. Still, the Wallers stated that the family prays together before dinner every night and when someone they know is sick.

Diamond Varner, who is American-born black and working class, and Karen Posner, who is white and lower class, said that they are religious and attend church regularly, but that their husbands do not attend nearly as much. Karen added that she finds that attending church with her children gives them all a chance to have "reflection time," and that it would be nice if Ted were included more than every once in a while. A similar description was captured in our field notes on the Wallers' (a white, middle-class couple) situation:

> Michelle said her husband's perspective on religion is that "you go to church, you take Communion, you say your prayers, you do what you're supposed to do in church and then you go home and forget about it until next Sunday." She then gives her own perspective in

saying, "it's something you have with you all the time, and if you can make it to church, you should."

Cameroonian Melea Spencer said her husband's excuse for not attending church (at least her Catholic one) is that he doesn't like an environment with "all that noise."[29] And while there are several other examples of the same ilk, there was only one case of the gender reverse: Donna Jones (white) said that it was her husband who was the more religious one. "I believe in the Lord, but I don't go to church. ... I would say, I guess I am a Christian?"

Some couples expressed disappointment in not aligning on religious matters, while others told us how disappointment can eventually lead to marital strain. This strain generally stems either from one spouse being uninterested in religious practice or from the spouses' practice of different faiths. In the cases of the American-born Erickson and Gardner couples, the husband chooses not to participate in church activities while the wife is actively and consistently engaged and frequently away from home as a result. Alena Chebet (Kenyan) said that while she and her husband strive to attend church regularly, she chooses not to attend unless her husband accompanies her. Here, his lack of participation in church with her is primarily because he follows another religious tradition. The Browns (white) also experience interfaith strain, manifest in their struggle to decide whether their children should be baptized as Catholics or Baptists. Alexis and Sean Abby (Ghanaian) said that they actually agree on so many essential issues like egalitarian marriage, the enjoyment of having children, and proactive financial security—but they have conflict over religious ideology. Alexis identifies as a Jehovah's Witness, where Sean prefers to call himself simply a "Christian." They see this issue as *the* biggest concern for them as a couple. This problem of navigating marriage and religion when "not on the same page" is of central concern for most such couples.

Though they represent only a few of the couples in our sample, the Jehovah's Witness couples stood out as particularly interesting in regard to their religious faith and marriage. For example, when only one partner is a Jehovah's Witness, marital strain seemed more pronounced compared to other interfaith couples. But where both partners are Jehovah's Witnesses, these couples spoke more openly and deeply than other religious couples on what they value about their shared faith and how their marriage is informed by it. We learned, for example, that the Greenes (white) had a rough first few years of marriage because the husband hadn't been "raised very religious" and had a lifestyle that was not compatible with the wife's beliefs. In time, however, they both came to appreciate that a Jehovah's Witness wife should have a nice home for her husband to come home to every day. And Michael Greene credited the Jehovah's Witnesses for helping him in managing marital and family conflict. Before joining the faith, he said he partied all the time and ran away from his problems, yelling at his kids rather than teaching them right and wrong more carefully. Now, he experiences married life more confident in his roles as husband and father.

Then there is Hank and Kelly Holmes' marriage (Caribbean), where its interfaith nature is only one dimension of the stress that plagues their relationship. A large portion of the stress comes from the business they co-own and the financial and managerial problems that have swamped their daily lives. The religious elements, however, are complex. Kelly explained that she was raised in the United States as a Southern Baptist but now describes her spiritual life as "metaphysical" and "Christian" with an incorporation of "Buddhist and Hindu philosophies." Hank's faith is the "Church of Jesus Christ," which given certain details of his description strongly suggests that he is a member of the Reorganized Church of Jesus Christ of Latter-day Saints (RLDS).[30] RLDS does not permit polygamy. Therefore, Kelly was likely referring to the religion Hank practiced back in Trinidad—the black Hebrew Israelites[31]—when she told us about her reservations in marrying a man whose religion encourages multiple marriages and views women as "possessions." Kelly expressed that when they met she was diametrically opposed to his religion's ethos but entered into marriage with him nonetheless, rushed into poor judgment by her ticking biological clock. The couple was still struggling with religious differences of some sort (and business-related stress) when we met them. They had legally separated but were still working and living together.

(In)Visibility Blues[32]

So, "is marriage for white people?" Of course not. But why young or older black people might sometimes ponder the question is quite evident from these discussions of social institutions and their influence on black marital life. The dearth of models of strong, black married life—or any black married life, for that matter—is taxing on black families and their communities, as are a wide array of socioeconomic challenges that persist to undermine many black couples who try their best to deliver on their vow to support one another. As is revealed in other parts of the text, most of the study couples are living happy lives despite all they must face on a daily basis. Many say they rely on religious or spiritual practice to help see them through. Others have found the struggle to reach or maintain stability a distraction from religious engagement.

Black immigrant couples focused their comments primarily on how their cultural approach to marriage and family differed from that of the American-born. But at times, there was empathy toward them or a least an understanding that life in America was uniquely difficult for those who have experienced racial and economic oppression over the full course of their lives, not to mention over their generations of ancestors. At times, whites also articulated a similar understanding, even while some of them delivered harsh criticisms of black marital life.

As is true for most other content reported in this text, we found little variation among these institutional themes based on the social-class status of the couples. Those from the middle class did contribute a bit more content overall in this section, and we suspect this is due to generally higher education and the greater exposure to the political discourse around institutional racism that it entails. But the slightly smaller amount of content offered by the working and lower classes did not translate into less comprehension, passion, or concern over the role that social institutions play in the disparate marital contexts of blacks and whites. Within and between the classes is a yearning for the public to recognize black marriage in all of its reality and complexity. One comes away from all of this realizing just how black marriages in our society are simultaneously hyper-visible and invisible.

Notes

1   Jones, Joy. 2006. "'Marriage Is for White People'." *Washington Post*, March 30. Retrieved May 27, 2007 (http://www.washingtonpost.com/ wp-dyn/content/article/2006/03/25/AR2006032500029.html).

2   Banks, Ralph Richard. 2011. *Is Marriage for White People?* New York: Plume.

3   Stanford Law School. 2016. "Is Marriage for White People?: How the African-American Marriage Decline Affects Everyone." Retrieved July 8, 2017 (http://ismarriageforwhite-people.stanford.edu/the-book/about-the-book/#).

4   McDonald, Katrina Bell. 2012. Book Review: *Is Marriage for White People? How the African-American Marriage Decline Affects Everyone* (by Banks, Richard R., 2011). *International Journal of Sociology of the Family* 38(1):121–123.

5   For example, see the work of Shirley Hill and Andrew Cherlin.

6   Hill, Shirley. 2012. *Families: A Social Class Perspective.* Thousand Oaks, CA: Sage Publications.

7   For a discussion of sexism, racism, and classism and how they can intersect, see McDonald, Katrina Bell. 1997. "The Psychosocial Dimension of Black Maternal Health: An Intersection of Race, Gender, and Class." Pp. 68–84 in *African Americans and the Public Agenda: The Paradoxes of Public Policy*, edited by Cedric Herring. New York: Russell Sage Foundation.

8   For a discussion of the "individualism–collectivism" dimension across cultures, see Hiew, Danika N. and W. Kim Halford. 2013. Pp. 87–99 in *Contemporary Issues in Family Studies: Global Perspectives on Partnerships, Parenting and Support in a Changing World*, edited by Angela Abela and Janet Walker. Oxford: John Wiley & Sons. Ltd.

9   For example, Alena Chebet says that she prefers the gender rights she enjoys in the United States as compared to her native Kenya. And Emmanuel Dawit says his relatives say he is "anti-Ethiopian" because he shuns the idea that he must be the dominant one in his marriage.

10 See Conrad, Cecelia. 2008. "Still Slipping: African-American Women in the Economy and in Society." *The American Prospect*. Retrieved August 24, 2017 (http://prospect.org/article/black-women-unfinished-agenda); and Glynn, Sarah Jane. 2016. "Breadwinning Mothers Are Increasingly the U.S. Norm." Retrieved August 24, 2017 (https://www.american-progress.org/issues/women/reports/2016/12/19/295203/breadwinning-mothers-are-increasingly-the-u-s-norm/).

11 Littlefield, Marci Bounds. 2008. "The Media as a System of Racialization Exploring Images of African American Women and the New Racism." *American Behavioral Scientist* 51(5): 675–685.

12 Mastro, Dana. 2015. "Why the Media's Role in Issues of Race and Ethnicity Should Be in the Spotlight." *Journal of Social Issues* 71(1):1–16.

13 For an excellent discussion of racial stereotypes, see Masuoka, Natalie, and Jane Junn. 2013. "The Pictures in Our Heads: The Content and Application of Racial Stereotypes." Pp. 63–87 in *The Politics of Belonging: Race, Public Opinion, and Immigration*. Chicago: University of Chicago Press.

14 Waller, James. 2001. *Face to Face: The Changing State of Racism Across America.* New York: Insight Books.

15 David Ayers quote taken from Waller, 2001, p. 29. From Ayers, David. 1993. *Social Psychology*, 4th ed. New York: McGraw Hill, p. 391.

16 This aspect of Bart McAllister's life is also highlighted in Chapter 4.

17 Dickson, Lynda. 1993. "The Future of Marriage and Family in Black America." *Journal of black Studies* 23(4):472–491.

18 In cases such as this, it was unclear whether whites were referring to all blacks or specifically the American-born.

19 Love, Bettina L., and Brandelyn Tosolt. 2010. "Reality or Rhetoric? Barack Obama and Post-racial America." *Race, Gender & Class* 17(3/4):19–37.

20 Love and Tosolt, 2010.

21 See, for example, the work of Eduardo Bonilla-Silva, numerous postings at the *Huffington Post*, and chatter on social media.

22 Hughey, Matthew W. 2014. "White Backlash in the 'Post-Racial' United States." *Ethnic and Racial Studies* 37(5):721–730; and Black, John. 2016. "This Is What 'Whitelash' Looks Like." *CNN.com*. Retrieved September 12, 2017 (http://www.cnn.com/2016/11/11/us/obama-trump-white-backlash/index.html).

23 Hughey, 2013.

24 Giddens, Anthony, Mitchell Duneier, Richard P. Applebaum, and Deborah Carr. 2009. *Introduction to Sociology*, 7th ed. New York: W. W. Norton & Company, Inc.

25 Giddens et al., 2009.

26 Saucier, Gerard, and Katarzyna Skrzypińska. 2006. "Spiritual But Not Religious? Evidence for Two Independent Dispositions." *Journal of Personality* 74(5):1257–1292.

27 There were several other incidences where either husbands or wives dismissed their religion's ideas on female submissiveness.

28 Goldenziel, Jill I. 2009. "Sanctioning Faith: Religion, State, and U.S.–Cuban Relations." *The Journal of Law & Politics* 25(2):179–210.

29 It should be noted that many contemporary African and African-American Catholic services have the spirited feel and sound of a typical black Baptist church.

30 See the following site for a description of the RLDS: http://eom.byu.edu/index.php/Reorganized_Church_of_Jesus_Christ_of_Latter_Day_Saints_(RLDS_Church)

31 For information on the black Hebrew Israelites, see https://www.washingtonpost.com/archive/local/1985/07/17/religious-sect-members-arrested-fbi-charges-25-black-hebrews-in-theft-and-fraud-schemes-in-dc-elsewhere/4fdd2f5c-0c73-488b-94e0-02bae6b4809a/?utm_term=.1ccfd5303bcf].

32 This heading is borrowed from McDonald, Katrina B., and Adia H. Wingfield. 2009. "(In)Visibility Blues: The Paradox of Institutional Racism." *Sociological Spectrum* 29:28–50. Here you will find a discussion of simultaneous "invisibility" and "visibility" as real and commonly experienced phenomena among blacks within predominantly white institutional settings.

7

SEX, MONEY, AND BEYOND

CONFLICT IN CONTEMPORARY
BLACK MARRIAGES

Roman and Ashley Barlow, a middle-class, American-born black couple, met at a bank where Ashley worked as a teller and Roman was a customer. Ashley said the first time she saw Roman, she thought, "That's him. I know that's him!" She gave him her phone number, they went out two nights in a row, and "that's been that." Although they agreed their meeting was a case of love at first sight, both brought plenty of baggage to the relationship. Ashley already had a daughter, and Roman's former partner was pregnant with his daughter. They'd each had some brushes with the law, and both had been involved in the drug trade—Ashley's former partner died when he swallowed balloons of heroin to escape charges in a drug bust. They conceived their son not long after they got together and had to create a home for their young children. But their biggest problem was their arguments— they both describe a steep learning curve for discovering how to have a good marriage. When they first got together, Ashley would say, "I'm leaving! I'm going to my mother's house!" whenever she got angry. It worked the first time, but soon Roman stopped reacting to the threat. He wouldn't fight with her, but they still weren't communicating. Gradually they began, as Ashley said, "learning more about each other, and basically trying to compromise and come together." Roman added, "We also talked a lot." Now, he told us, "Once or twice a week, we have our moments where we'll sit and talk

for a few hours … We have a policy to not go to bed angry."Ashley added,
"We stick together about anything."

Marital Conflict

Experiencing conflict is a universal aspect of being human. People disagree about policies in their workplaces, laws put in place by their govern-
ments, and rules at their schools. People also disagree with each other.
Some sociological theories assume that all interactions among people
are based around conflict. Sociological theorists beginning with Engels
and Durkheim believed that what happens in the family is a microcosm
of what happens in an entire society. Others, such as Erving Goffman,
have focused more on interaction between individuals, considering who
has more power in relationships and how people respond when they
don't agree. But all agree that conflict in families—particularly between
husbands and wives—is important to understanding both families
and society.[1]

The "honeymoon period" of Ashley and Roman's relationship, like so
many relationships among black couples, was marred by conflict, especially their different styles of managing it, something that was mirrored
in many of our couples. Researchers frequently put a person's conflict
management style into one of three buckets: constructive, destructive,
or withdrawal.[2] Ashley's original style was destructive: She yelled and
whined, criticizing Roman as mean and unreasonable, threatening to
leave him. Roman responded by withdrawing, sitting on the couch reading, and ignoring Ashley's barbs. As Ashley said to Roman, reflecting on
their early years, "I wanted to argue, and you wouldn't want to argue."
People's conflict styles often remain consistent over time, so problems with
conflict early in a relationship can predict what will come throughout a
marriage, and some research shows that black couples begin marriage at
a disadvantage in the conflict department.[3] For instance, black couples
are more likely than white couples to be low income and have children
from other relationships, stressors that are noted as frequent sources of
marital conflict.[4] Researchers have used analysis of conflict styles along
with personal situations and social structures to explain higher rates of
divorce among black couples. But this study isn't looking at couples who

divorced, it's looking at couples who remained married and were, for the most part, trying to work things out. Some did maintain conflict patterns that seemed to perpetuate, rather than resolve, their problems. But more often, like Roman and Ashley, couples who began with ineffective conflict management developed more constructive approaches over time.

Some couples get along well day to day, while others seem like they argue about everything, from who should clean the toothpaste splatters off the bathroom mirror to who ate the last slice of cold pizza. According to research on marital conflicts, among couples with children, children are at the root of many disagreements, but all couples also commonly have conflicts over chores, communication, leisure time, work, money, personal habits, and other family members. Studies show that these topics are similar across couples from all kinds of backgrounds and are reported fairly equally among both husbands and wives.[5]

Sometimes outside factors place stress on couples and their families, such as unemployment, criminal justice policies, or housing costs. No husband or wife sets the country's legal policy or controls the national economy, but national and local politics and economics can still create conflicts in families. So can policies set by other institutions in a couple's life, such as their church or their children's school. Institutions and the conflicts they can generate for black marriages are discussed in-depth in Chapter 6, while this chapter will focus on interpersonal conflict.

A Social Policy Approach to Healthy Marriage

In 1996, as part of its national welfare reform initiative, the federal government under the Clinton administration began to focus on "healthy marriage" as a way to strengthen family ties. The goal was to reduce use of public assistance programs by encouraging lower-income couples to get married and stay married.[6] Under the George W. Bush administration, in 2005 the federal Office of Family Assistance, a division of the Administration for Children and Families, began offering grants specifically to promote "healthy marriage."[7] As noted in Chapter 2, families headed by stably married couples tend to offer benefits to both couples and children: Household incomes are higher in families headed by married couples, both husbands and wives tend to be physically and emotionally healthier, and children are usually better off.[8] Regardless of income, children in "complex families," those where there are children from multiple relationships and adults may rotate in and out, fare worse in their relationships with their families, their health and well-being, and their educational achievement than children of stably married parents.[9] Marriage is more than just the sum of its parts, and families benefit from the increased stability and flexibility marriage can bring to income, housing, social networks, and available time to spend with children and do household work.[10] Children, however, often flounder when their parents are in high-conflict marriages,[11] and when conflict cannot be resolved, divorce can wreak havoc on all family members, emotionally and economically.[12] Thus, it is not a marriage ceremony alone that is important to strengthening families, but sustaining marriages that are "healthy."

The Healthy Marriage Initiative defines healthy marriage as a mutually enriching relationship in which both spouses have a deep respect for each other. The initiative's description also states that healthy marriage "is a mutually satisfying relationship that is beneficial to the husband, wife and children (if present)" and "a relationship that is committed to ongoing growth, the use of effective communication skills and the use of successful conflict management skills."[13] Given the role of conflict in breaking up relationships either before or after marriage, it is not surprising that conflict management and communication skills were emphasized as key components of promoting healthy marriage.

Despite what sometimes seems like a relentless media focus on how black families differ from white families, much of the family therapy and other literature on communication and conflict resolution has tried to find a one-size-fits-all approach that gives little or no attention to racial, cultural, or economic differences among couples. Many marriage education programs are driven by findings from researchers such as John and Julie Gottman,[14] who identified "Four Horsemen of the Apocalypse" that they said doomed marriages: criticism, defensiveness, contempt, and stonewalling. They generalized from findings based on mostly white couples studied primarily in the 1970s to potential therapeutic interventions intended to apply to all couples in an increasingly diverse and quickly evolving society. We are not the only scholars to question marriage support programs that apply findings from white, middle-class couples to lower-income couples or couples of color.[15] While certainly we did not observe criticism, defensiveness, contempt, or stonewalling to be healthy mechanisms among our couples, we did see different patterns of behavior, values, and coping among couples, patterns that influenced their own perceptions of the health of their marriages. Here we discuss patterns that emerged among our couples—both those that appeared near-universal and ones that were more apparent among individuals or couples from particular backgrounds, whether by race, class, or culture, as well as differences by gender.

Conflict among the Contemporary Black Marriage Study Couples

Conflict existed among all of the couples we interviewed. Among some, conflict was barely noticeable because the husband and wife handled their differences constructively, working through their issues together and arriving at mutually agreeable solutions. Some spouses were destructive in approaching conflicts, raising their voices and treating their significant other with contempt. Still others withdrew, refusing to argue, even leaving the house when a conflict arose. Often one spouse was destructive while the other withdrew, and within couples, husbands and wives sometimes traded these styles back and forth. Even though conflict is nearly universal in marriages, some couples were surprised that marriage didn't end with "happily ever after." As Aretha Washington, a middle-class, American-born black wife, said,

> I know everything is not going to be perfect. But I [was] always as a teenager saying I would be glad when I get my time to go from all this fighting and fussing [with my boyfriend]. I always figure everything is just happy in the marriage. I know that that's not true, but that's how I always looked at it.

But our couples had all been married at least five years, and while conflict strategies usually did not undergo a complete transformation, most of our couples reported that they had learned and were applying more productive conflict management as the years went by.

Frequent sources of conflict among our couples were similar to those observed in research on marriage: children, chores, communication, sex and fidelity, leisure time, work, money, addiction, personal habits, and other family members. Some issues, particularly those related to chores, work, leisure time, and children, have been discussed in previous chapters. Unlike most of the couples in those chapters and in our study, Roman and Ashley's relationship was egalitarian in both ideals and practice. Roman worked from home doing financial consulting, while Ashley worked in a store downtown and had a side business selling custom-designed clothes she made. Roman, who valued egalitarianism already, took on many household and childcare tasks without a thought. The two liked to keep their condominium clean, but if anything, Roman was more likely to stay on top of the daily grind of vacuuming, dishwashing, and laundry because he was at home. They occasionally quarreled about clutter, but for the most part, sharing kept conflict at bay. But Roman and Ashley were unusual in that department.

As noted in Chapters 4 and 5, it was common for wives to feel over-burdened by childrearing and household tasks. Even when wives did not expect—or even desire—an equal division of labor, they often wished their husbands offered more "help." Women across classes, races, and countries of origin often felt their husbands did not recognize or appreciate their chore burdens. Men only rarely spoke of being burdened by chores relative to their wives, and wives often carried a resentment over imbalances in responsibilities for chores and children relative to leisure time, even when the wives accepted the imbalance as normal. As with Roman and Ashley, the more they learned to share, the less conflict they had about these issues.

Money

Roman told us that, in his vision of an ideal marriage, "You never worry about money." We didn't seem to have a single couple who met that ideal. Money was mentioned by the vast majority of couples as a source of conflict regardless of the family's race, country of origin, gender, or even the couple's financial stability. Some couples with low education were chronically on the brink of economic disaster; other couples were striving to get out from under debt resulting from student loans or a catastrophic event. But many better-off couples were also in debt and had trouble explaining why. Couples who appeared to have sufficient income to maintain a middle-class lifestyle that included a home, cars, and all the necessities of daily living often complained of credit cards maxed out on collections of small purchases, such as video games or multiple pairs of children's shoes. As Roman noted of his family's spending, "We'll have spurts where, you know, 10, 15 here, 10, 15 there, 10, 15 here, 20 there, and all of a sudden [it's a thousand bucks], you know?" Many couples included both a spouse who embraced spending and one who valued saving—with both roles distributed fairly equally among husbands and wives. The saver was universally frustrated by the free-spending spouse, while the spender was more likely to feel misunderstood, a situation ripe for criticism from the saver and defensiveness on the part of the spender.

Some couples mentioned financial conflicts as peaking early in their marriages but resolving over time. Roman said that when they met, Ashley was "always used to getting her way," and she agrees: "I wasn't used to having a man tell me no." When Ashley wanted to go shopping shortly after they married and Roman didn't want her to, he said, "She lost it, and she threw a temper tantrum [and I thought], Oh my God, what have I done?" But Ashley loved their spacious, tastefully decorated condo and was excited about the prospect of sending their older daughter to a private high school. After Roman consistently ignored her tantrums, she stopped having them and gradually came around to accept that his money management skills were getting her family where she wanted it to be. Roman said that marriage had enhanced financial stability for both of them.

Destiny and Terrell, another American-born black couple whom we met in Chapter 4, also found their values on money management coming together. A few years before we met them, they had nearly split up because of Terrell's wild spending and Destiny's reluctance to be the killjoy who reined it in—until they went bankrupt. During his individual interview, Terrell talked about being in high school and the status that came from having the latest "tennies," but he emphasized how much he had changed, learning that material things don't matter, people do—especially Destiny. Now, he said, high school acquaintances were surprised to see him driving "an old car," but he and Destiny faced financial conflicts constructively now, rather than both withdrawing as they used to. Involving himself more in the family's finances and considering the needs of Destiny and their children brought Terrell around to becoming a saver himself.

The Buckleys, a middle-class couple from Sudan, reduced conflict over money for very different reasons. For Kenneth Buckley, coming to terms with his wife's shopping habits was not only a way to keep the peace, but also a justification to watch soccer matches on television as he pleased, something his wife resented:

> Right now, my first thing is just to go and watch the game. I don't want to go online, I didn't listen to the news 'cause I want to watch it! I can accept [her going out with a friend shopping]. Totally, when out of the blue she's broke and she's borrowing money, and I'm thinking, why does someone have to ask for money so she can go shopping? If you don't have money, don't shop. And I will accept that, but she'll never accept that I am going on Sunday to watch a game.

Rather than coming together with his wife on values regarding money, Kenneth felt that accepting his wife's spending should be a bargaining chip for his own leisure time, which he could then take without apology. But his acceptance did reduce their conflicts over money.

Some couples' money conflicts were frequent and ongoing. Though either a husband or wife could get ticked off about rising household debt and what they saw as their spouse's unnecessary spending, only wives ever stated that their spouse's spending habits put the well-being of their family in jeopardy. James and Mia Davis, the working-class Caribbean couple we met in Chapter 5, were underwater not only because of James' child support payments, but also because he would take what little was left over and buy a round of drinks for friends at the bar. Being popular overshadowed paying the rent. Mia, who believed their religious and cultural values dictated that he must remain in charge of their money, felt financial stress ooze into every interaction. She withdrew further and further, including in their bedroom, where their sex life was nearly dead. She seemed, with great sadness, to view James with contempt.

Eric and Diamond Varner, a working-class, American-born black couple, had similar issues. He did construction and she was in sales, and with a recent promotion, she saw her income nearly double. Still, they couldn't seem to make ends meet—because of Eric. Diamond says,

> [E]ven when I wasn't making much money, I was responsible enough to pay the bills first. And I guess with Eric seeing that, he knew that things were going to get paid anyway and he would take his money and go party. He parties. I mean I'm not saying he didn't pay anything, I was just more responsible than him. I should have a house; I make good money. But anyways, all the bills and things got piled up on me—I'm the responsible one that pays the bills. Of course things get behind—we have the truck note and insurance and rent and different things and the kids. So I'm pretty much playing catch up now—not even catch up, you know?

Diamond later revealed that she also suspected Eric might be helping to support a second family that he had never revealed to her. Their method of dealing with their money conflict switched between confrontation and withdrawal. The two argued vigorously, which was glaringly apparent in their joint interview, where they had several spirited back-and-forths on money, their division of labor, and responsibility for their three daughters. But Diamond said of conflicts with Eric, "He leaves [when we argue]. I can't stand that. If you're mad, just talk to me please. [Walking out] is so much worse than just arguing with me." At the same time, Eric's lack of investment in their family led Diamond to check out emotionally. She said she now regards him as more of a companion than a spouse, and they too have a dead sex life.

Even couples who agreed about money could find it a source of tension because, for most, there was never enough of it. Charles and Keisha Parrish, a working-class, American-born black couple, were both spenders and agreed that they have "a shopping addiction." Keisha left public assistance after a brief stint because having both of them in the workforce gave them better cash flow. They avoided credit cards, but even though they agreed that they would be better off if both of them "shopped like normal people," they were always short on funds.

Some couples were financially unstable because one member of the couple was not employed. Among couples with a mother caring for children full-time, agreement that this was an ideal arrangement did not shield the couple from financial stress. In other couples, when one partner (usually the husband) could not find a stable job, the couple understood that a floundering economy and discrimination in the job market against black men or men with a criminal record were primarily responsible—but again, that didn't lessen the tension of living hand-to-mouth. Couples in these situations didn't respond to each other with any of the Gottmans' apocalyptic horsemen when it came to money, but heightened tension could lead to snowballing conflict over all kinds of issues. As Taylor McCoy, a Caribbean wife in a struggling working-class family, noted,

> Gabriel does all that he can for us. And we see it. And we do appreciate it. But it's the economics just makes it harder for him to do what he's supposed to do. I'm not asking to be rich … just to be comfortable. Not to have to worry about rent next month, you can't take off, we can't go nowhere because we gotta work every single day.

In a few cases, money problems were caused or compounded by a spouse's addiction. Though we spoke with a number of Caribbean or American-born black husbands who confessed to drug dealing in their younger days, most were not addicted. Drug dealing was a source of income, and the men stopped because of fear of going to prison, usually citing their marriages and children as keeping them on the straight and narrow. On the other hand, Bart and Lori McAllister, an American-born black couple scraping by on her minimum-wage salary and some state assistance Bart received for his son, didn't have the funds to turn on their heat as December grew colder and colder. But Lori always had enough money for beer, and she resisted any suggestion by Bart that she stop at one. Because only she earned a steady income, he felt helpless to protest. Mike Thompson, a lower-class white husband, did well for himself as a professional athlete in his twenties, but his drug addiction ultimately sucked away every penny. He tried giving up heroin after he couldn't fully participate in the birth of his older son because he was high.

He was in a period of sobriety when we first met him, but as he and his wife Laura (also white) journaled for the next few months, they reported on Mike's job troubles, the death of his grandmother, and problems in parenting Laura's teenage daughter. Money again began disappearing as Mike resumed his drug habit. Harold and Bethany Wilcox, a working-class white couple, reported that Harold's gambling addiction nearly split them up. Harold, who had also been a professional athlete, didn't go into debt but spent all money that didn't go to necessities on gambling. After Bethany took their son and moved out, he began attending Gamblers Anonymous, and they reconciled. At the time of the interview they lived below their means, choosing to stay in a well-kept trailer rather than buy a suburban tract home.

We did have some additional couples with a spouse struggling with addiction where the addiction was not tied specifically to money conflicts, but overall we did not have enough couples confronting addiction to make any generalizations about patterns in the ways couples addressed it. It is likely that a larger sample would reveal attitudes and behavior that vary somewhat based on social class, education, race, or cultural backgrounds. We also observed only couples who remained married, not couples who confronted addiction and then divorced. Addiction's role in marriage and conflict—especially among black couples—should be further studied.

Children and Blended Families

Daily conflicts over children were common among all couples who were parents. As discussed in Chapter 5, almost all of our couples had children at home, and conflicts were especially frequent in regard to discipline (one parent often felt that the other was too strict or too soft) and the daily slog of child-related chores (which burdened women disproportionately). When it came to stepchildren, however, we noticed sharp differences among our couples. About a third of our couples involved stepchildren, and though the number of families with stepchildren was small for the groups other than the American-born blacks, the level and type of conflict stepchildren generated differed starkly by race and country of origin.

Half of the American-born black couples we interviewed included children from at least one spouse's previous relationships. These children nearly always lived with the couple at least part-time, if not full-time. Though a number of couples noted conflicts with a spouse's previous partner, few noted conflicts with or about the children themselves. American-born blacks often embrace extended kin networks—meaning extended networks of family and friends beyond their own spouse and children. Being less focused on the nuclear family has sometimes been leveled as a criticism against black families, assumed to mean that their families are less stable and committed. But other research shows that tighter extended kin networks, when they exist, can be supportive for adults[16] and give children better resiliency.[17]

In general, black spouses embraced each other's children as their own—or close to it. Roman and Ashley barely distinguished genetic relationships with their three children—biologically their older daughter, Michelle, is hers and the younger, DeeDee, is his. Their youngest child, Isaiah, they had together. Because Michelle's biological father is deceased, Roman has been able to legally adopt her. As for DeeDee, Roman had split up with her mother and was already seeing Ashley when DeeDee was born. Roman and his ex had an informal custody arrangement, but DeeDee came over every school day because she and Isaiah attended the same school and Roman drove them. She stayed in the afternoon to do homework and sometimes spent nights or weekends. Both Roman and Ashley seemed genuinely content for DeeDee to be over as much as she liked—the only conflict they mentioned was with DeeDee's mother, who resented Roman for leaving her and didn't get along with Ashley.

Ruth and Elijah Martin, a working-class, American-born black couple, have a daughter together and also have full custody of Elijah's son from a prior marriage, Elijah Junior. Ruth hasn't adopted E.J., but she chuckled lovingly as she described building her relationship with him after he met her and began calling her Ms. Ruth: "I didn't wanna tell him to call me Mom. I wanted that to be his decision." She got him to drop the Ms., then to call her by a family nickname, Ree. Finally, she said,

We was all sitting around for brunch and I said, "Look, aren't you tired of calling me Ree?" And he was like, "Yeah," and I said, "Well what you wanna call me?" and he just get this smirk ... I said, "Do you wanna call me Mom?" And he was like, "Yeah." And I said, "Why didn't you just say that?" and he said, "I don't know." ... So then after that, now he calls me Mom.

Like Roman, Ashley, and Ruth, most American-born black spouses viewed all the children living in their home as their children, regardless of the biological relationship. They also welcomed visits from non-custodial children and often had informal custody arrangements that worked well even if the couple was not on good terms with the ex-partner. Children were children, and conflict was reserved for adults.

Among Caribbean couples we interviewed, only husbands had children from previous relationships, and for the most part, this caused little if any conflict because these children were entirely absent from the couples' life. Even though Caribbeans are known for embracing extended kin networks, the matrifocality of Caribbean culture meant the children remained connected almost solely with their mothers. In the case of Kylie and Odell Velarde, Odell's children from his previous relationship were already adults themselves and still lived in Cuba. Gabriel McCoy also had two sons, also older, whom he never saw. No Caribbean wives reported an expectation that they make any social investment in the husband's children from other relationships. The only couple who experienced significant conflict over the husband's other children were James and Mia, who weren't really in conflict about the children themselves but about James' deception about how many children he had and his hefty child support payments. In a telling statement regarding how socially and emotionally disengaged James was from the children he had before meeting Mia, he spoke longingly of having a son, with no apparent recognition that he already had one.

Three working-class couples with an African husband and American-born black wife involved stepchildren. In two cases, the wife had a child from a previous relationship who lived with the couple and the couple also had a child together, but in neither case did the husband bring up issues with having a stepchild. In both cases, the husband left primary parenting to the wife, and having a stepchild produced no conflict. The third couple, Travon and Abeni Sesay, have no children together. Her daughter from a previous relationship lived with them, but they were also anticipating the arrival of Travon's two sons, who had been living with their mother in Cameroon. Abeni was relieved that the mounds of immigration paperwork were complete and was ready to welcome the boys as brothers to her daughter. Like many American-born black spouses, she voiced nothing but pleasure at the prospect of having stepchildren join their family, saying,

> I am excited about his two boys coming from Africa. I want them to come here and have a good life and be around their father. ... I can't wait. He is excited because he hasn't been around his kids.

Among white couples, every family with stepchildren discussed ongoing conflict around those children. Conflict regarding the ex-partner was sometimes projected onto the child as well. The most extreme case of conflict we saw was between William and Lynne Brown, a working-class couple who had two daughters together, Brittany and Sophia. Will's daughter from a previous relationship, Allison, spent weekends and much of the summer with them, and Lynne had nothing but resentment toward her. Will said the conflict began after Brittany was born, after which Lynne began viewing Allison, age 3 at the time, as competition for resources for Brittany:

> Even while Lynne was pregnant, everything was fine. But once Lynne had the first kid, that's when everything changed with the jealousy factor. It was like, "You're paying child support, so why don't you put some money out on Brittany?" And you know, all right, I'm paying $100 [for Allison] a week, so why don't you spend that on [Brittany]?

Lynne wanted to make sure Brittany and Sophia got as much or more than Allison did, from the number of Christmas presents to pairs of shoes. Will says of conflict over Allison, "That's 90 percent of our fight. And it's 90 percent of things that get thrown up in my face." For her part, Lynne insisted she just wanted Will to treat the three girls the same. Every couple she knows with stepchildren has problems, and she said that if she were to have a do-over,

I would never marry a guy with another kid. Even if they were 12 [years old], never. I don't care how much money they have. I wouldn't do it, just because of the simple fact of what I've been through in this.

For white families, stepchildren were not absorbed into the marriage as a joint resource but rather were a sign of the couples' past lives and their differences. Money and other resources spent on a child were, for the non-biological parent, taking away from resources that could be going toward the marriage and the children the couple had together. As Will said, "We're both going to have different outlooks on it, because Allison's mine, and she ain't Lynne's."

Unlike most issues we explored, when it came to stepchildren, we found remarkable consistency within race and immigrant groups and stark differences between them. However, because the number of step-families was limited, these findings indicate a need for further exploration rather than a definitive explanation. Stepfamilies were not represented among middle-class couples with the exception of the Barlows, so considering differences by class may be important within and among black couples from different backgrounds.

Sex While Married

Some of our couples spoke highly of their sexual relationships, but many had small children at home, and small children are generally not helpful to a couple's sex life. Some of our couples despaired over not having enough time for each other inside or outside the bedroom. Sometimes a husband complained his wife's interest in sex diminished with the birth of a child. Sometimes couples just found their levels of desire to be mismatched. And life got in the way, as with Jefferson Lewis, who is Caribbean, and his wife Jasmine, who is American-born black. The Lewises are middle-class parents of two boys, and when they were interviewed Jeff was unemployed, and Jasmine was exhausted from holding down a full-time job on top of remaining responsible for much of the household work. Jeff complained that their sex life was stale to the point that he sometimes fantasized about being with someone else (something he hadn't acted upon). Jasmine said that experimenting in the bedroom made her feel "a bit silly," but the biggest problem was that Jeff wanted to try "something new" at three o'clock in the morning when she was dead tired.

Even when the church weighed in, couples generally went their own way regarding sex, whether that was having premarital sex, extramarital sex, or no sex. Aretha Washington told us,

> And, [the Bible] also says ... your body don't belong to you anymore, and I don't follow that. My bishop tells me that all the time. Your body don't belong to you no more. It's [your husband's], and whatever he wants, you know, he can take it and it's not considered rape. You know, even though it wouldn't get to that point. ... He know not to even go there with me.

Like the Lewises, many couples weren't always satisfied with their sex lives but still seemed to muddle through the ups and downs of sex in marriage. What most impacted relationships was acting on fantasies of being unfaithful.

Estimates of infidelity rates in marriages vary wildly. People may be more or less likely to admit to having an affair depending on how the question is asked, with people less likely to confess to infidelity in face-to-face interviews (such as the ones we conducted) than on computer-assisted surveys.[18] Most estimates of infidelity consider the life of the marriage, with estimates ranging from as low as 10% for wives and 20% for husbands to rates much higher—and sometimes almost identical—for both.[19] At any given period, few spouses admit to infidelity during the previous year—around 2%.[20] Though there is an overall low incidence of active infidelity at any particular point in time, rates of infidelity are often thought to vary by race and class status. Stereotypes used to dehumanize black Americans and justify race-based discrimination often pointed to voracious sexual appetites among both men and women as evidence of an animalistic nature.[21] Literature on Caribbean men indicates that infidelity is common and often tolerated as an expression of masculinity,[22] and though polygyny in Africa is declining, it still remains a common practice.[23] However, research investigating racial and ethnic differences in infidelity is mixed, with clear indications that different cultures around the world have different attitudes about extramarital sex, but that affairs are not necessarily more common among American blacks than among Americans of other racial–ethnic groups. Regarding class, when differences are observed, those who are higher income or have more education appear more likely to have extramarital sex than those who are lower income or less educated.[24] Little research has investigated the intersections of race, gender, class, and culture that would be relevant to the couples we met.

Being unfaithful, confronting a partner's infidelity, or just worrying about a partner's infidelity were all circumstances our couples confronted, and all three issues impacted both husbands and wives. Part of Ashley and Roman's closeness has stemmed not only from the fact that each was faithful to the other, but that both of them had complete trust in each other's fidelity. Fidelity was directly connected to love and trust for many couples. For instance, Erin Larson, a white working-class wife originally from Puerto Rico, suffered from chronic pain than sometimes precluded sexual intimacy. Her husband Alex, who is white and mainland born, said that he married her because "there was a very powerful trust we had there." He emphasized the importance of remaining faithful despite Erin's limitations:

> We both really want to be with each other, but we can't right now, because she's sick or vice-versa. I can see where it would be really easy for someone else to say, "You know what, she's sick, I don't care; I'm gonna go stag, because the opportunity is there so I'm gonna go and do something with someone else." I don't do that. I love that woman.

Despite the research that shows infidelity rises with education and income, deep trust was most common among middle-class couples we interviewed. But we saw both deep trust and mistrust among couples across the class spectrum.

A number of spouses confessed to infidelity during their interviews. Sometimes the affairs were secret, and in such cases, the unfaithful spouse was often seeking to *avoid* conflict—not just about the affair, but about other issues in the marriage. Hannah Dewit, a middle-class, American-born black wife married to an African immigrant, had an affair in part because of her husband's anger and controlling behavior. When he began treating her with more respect, she cut off the affair, but she never told him about it. In her case, rather than causing conflict, the affair was a way to withdraw from conflict. As the marriage became a safer space, Hannah recommitted herself to it. Ron Washington, a middle-class, American-born black husband, also used infidelity to avoid conflict. His wife Aretha was upfront about not enjoying sex, rejecting Ron's advances even under orders from their church bishop to engage. In his individual interview, Ron revealed,

> I'm affectionate. I have a very high sexual appetite. She really doesn't. She has tried to change here and there, but it's still pretty much the same. And I knew when I met her. ... I felt like as the years have gone on that it would change, but you know.

He said Aretha responded to his sexual interest by saying, "You're a freak!" so he turned to other women for a sexual outlet. As for Aretha's knowledge of his affairs, he said, "She just knows there was a female ..." but thought that the relationship "was just conversation." From Ron's vantage point, an occasional affair allowed him to remain dedicated to his wife. He said, "I'm always trying to make sure I let her know whenever I can. Just let her know she knows she's loved no matter what." Overall, middle-class spouses were most likely to keep affairs secret.

In other cases, a husband or wife knew about a spouse's affair—or affairs. Taylor McCoy told us that if Gabriel wanted to have sex with another woman, she might not like it, but what was most important was that he be open and honest with her rather than sneaking around. But for couples who put that idea into practice, the openness was generally not helpful to the relationship. One exception was the most mild of cases. Alex Larson, who as stated above valued being faithful to his wife, also told us, "I'll go out with some friends and ... one of those places might have been a strip club. I'm not going to hide the fact that I went to a strip club." Erin wasn't thrilled about his dalliances, but she said, "He lets me know, 'This is what we're doing,' and I'm like, 'Okay, just don't touch her!'" Alex saw his communication as "conflict resolution," and added, "It'll go as far as she trusts me and I trust her." But Alex wasn't planning on emotionally investing in anyone outside the marriage or in having intimate sexual relations.

Other spouses went much further, with devastating results. Mariah Rowe, a lower-class, American-born black wife, has had affair partners that have included Jonathan's brother and the woman who lives next door. Jonathan even engaged in three-way sex with Mariah and the neighbor to try to please Mariah, but in his individual interview, he told us that Mariah doesn't respect him anymore and complains to him "that I can't go as long as I used to." He rationalized her affairs as his fault for not satisfying her: "I mean, you know when you can't get it, I mean as far as when you at home, then you go other places." But her affairs were making their sex life worse. Jonathan said,

> Her and my brother had an affair and until this very day, I know they still are. And she probably say, well me not satisfying her the way that she would want to be. I mean, it takes more interest out of me. Sometime when I'm with her and we be laying there with each other, I be like I don't even want to do this, you know? And then one time we went weeks and weeks without even touching each other.

Mariah wasn't employed at the time of the interview, and Jonathan worried constantly that she was stepping out on him "whenever she goes somewhere." Jonathan said, "I'm always catching her in lies and all types of things," such as saying she's seeing a friend, but when he checked the car mileage, he found she didn't drive far enough to see that friend. When Jonathan tried to address his feelings with Mariah, "It ends up screaming and hollering," so instead, he withdrew from conflicts, not only by curtailing their sex life but by not engaging in arguments. He said rather than "catching an attitude," now they "drop or put all of our hard feelings aside and it would go back to normal … just like ain't nothin' happen." In her individual interview, Mariah explained that "I love Jonathan, but I'm not in love with him anymore." She said of her infidelities, "I guess I was just looking for something better than I had 'cause I was bored," but she resented that Jonathan was always suspicious of her and thought that he has also had affairs. Jonathan said that he didn't leave Mariah because "when you be in a relationship with somebody for that long, it's hard to just stop."

In another case of flagrant infidelity, Charles Parrish, the husband in the couple with the shopping addiction, openly had affairs and has had children with other women while in his relationship with Keisha. Keisha found out about children with one of the women when Charles dropped the older child off for Keisha to babysit while his girlfriend gave birth to their second child. When interviewed, he said he was completely open with Keisha now, saying,

> Keisha is probably my best friend in the entire world. 'Cause it don't matter what it is, if it's drugs, if it's other females, if it's this or whatever it is, I can just go and talk to her ... yeah, she might get some feelings or whatever ... but if I'm coming and telling her, "Look, I don't know why I mess with this chick," she'll listen.

But at this point, Charles said that he and Keisha "don't really deal in romance," and Keisha said, "he has this little chick that he's still dealing with, so I'm putting myself on strike" regarding sex. Charles identified "my infidelity" as the biggest problem in their marriage. Charles said it's too hard to stop being unfaithful, especially since he no longer gets high on drugs, but Keisha responded, "It isn't hard." As with Jonathan and Mariah, discussing the matter directly led to destructive conflict, and Keisha in particular primarily dealt with the issue by withdrawing from it—including withdrawing from their sex life.

Just worrying that a spouse has had an affair can wreak havoc on a couple's relationship, whether or not an affair actually happened.[25] Samantha Trotter, a middle-class Caribbean wife, went through a deep depression a few years before the interview, and her husband Ryan, who is American-born black, said he suspected she stepped out on him during this period. During these years, he considered walking away, but he had nowhere to go except back with his parents, whom he doesn't enjoy spending time with, so he stayed. As for Sam, she claimed not to remember what she did during her period of depression, though she did remember "reaching out to old friends from back home." Ryan's suspicions constantly lurked beneath the surface. He worried that Sam viewed sex with him like an item on a checklist: did the grocery shopping, washed the dishes, had sex with Ryan. He would think about having an affair to see if he could make another woman happy.

Lynne and Will Brown's conflict was louder. In addition to constant arguments over Will's daughter Allison, there was Allison's mother—Lynne worried that Will might still be interested in her. Lynne was possessive and had fits of jealousy whenever Will went out on his own. She developed elaborate schemes to check up on him, making calls and pretending to be other people. She threatened him with what she would do if he ever cheated on her:

> if anything happens I'm going to hit you hard. I'm going to get child support. Like, I'm not going to do verbal like [Allison's mother]. I'm going to a lawyer. I want full custody of the kids. I want visitation rights, you can have visitation rights, but I want it supervised with both parents.

She even packed up their daughters and left once for a few days. Lynne knew her destructive behavior scared Will, and she believed it kept him on the straight and narrow. But the fear also kept Will on edge, and he withdrew, which prevented them from having honest communication.

Neither American-born whites nor blacks approved of extramarital sex for their spouses—some might tolerate it, but they didn't like it or think of it as acceptable. As noted at the beginning of this section, extramarital relations for men are common and often expected in the Caribbean, and polygyny is still practiced throughout much of Africa. We saw extramarital sex normalized—only for men—among some of our Caribbean or African couples, as when Taylor McCoy said, "It's common for a man with multiple wives, multiple women, that's very common in the Caribbean." Kylie Velarde told us that she preferred having an older husband (Odell is fifteen years her senior) because an older man was less likely to pursue other women. She was pleased that the only time Odell had stepped out on her was during her pregnancy, and he did not pick up a sexually transmitted infection. Rahim Yabu, a working-class husband originally from Sierra Leone, spoke positively about the role of polygyny in his home country:

In terms of marriage ... once over there, in the Third World country
... I can have two, three wives at the same time, as long as I can provide and take care of them. But the kids, they all grow up together,
the same roof, they all come up, the mothers get along very good.
Then when they grow up, each and everyone know each other and
love each other.

Still, though couples acknowledged that extramarital relations for men
were common practice and culturally accepted, most Caribbean and
African wives were less than enthusiastic about husbands engaging in
such relations. Morgan Peterson, a middle-class Caribbean wife, wrote
almost sixty journal entries mourning her husband's infidelities, saying
she only stayed in the marriage because of her religious beliefs. Alena
Chebet, a middle-class wife from Kenya, said she does not want to return
to Africa despite the fact that she generally prefers Kenyan life, especially
for the values it would transmit to her children. Her reason was that
many of her friends back home have husbands who have taken second
wives. She wanted to make sure Danny had no such option, which she
felt she could only enforce by staying in the United States. Just because
extramarital sex for men was normalized in their home countries didn't
mean Caribbean and African immigrant wives weren't bothered by it or
wanted to accept it.

Affairs are more common in relationships that are low quality, but
affairs also lower the quality of relationships.[26] Infidelity is a common
reason for divorce.[27] Our couples may have been more likely than average to be faithful (or to have successfully hidden their infidelities), which
may have been among the reasons that they had remained married. No
spouse who knew of a partner's infidelity was happy with their marriage,
and some, such as the Rowes, may have been heading for an ultimate
divorce. Couples who trusted each other implicitly were among the hap-
piest couples, regardless of gender, race, class, or country of origin.

Us Against Them: Managing Extended Family Conflicts

If there's one thing that drove Ashley and Roman Barlow crazy, it was
their families—both complained about their parents and siblings and
seemed to feel their extended families brought little benefit to their lives.

Ashley said that the hardest thing about marriage was, "[d]ealing with your parents and siblings and having them trying to put their two cents into your marriage and what should be going on, and we have a lot of that." Roman reminisced about a period when they lived in another part of the state, away from extended family: "That was the biggest thing that I loved about living down there. It was just us. We didn't have to deal with her parents." He added, "With me, with my parents, I've kind of pushed my parents off to a good degree. Because I mean initially when we first got married … my mom could not stand Ashley."

Some couples expressed admiration for their parents' relationships, but others specifically did not want to be like their parents. As mentioned in Chapter 4, a number of African spouses commented that they didn't like the way their fathers behaved as "dictators," and they wanted to have more collaborative relationships with their own spouses. Others saw other conflict-generating behaviors that that they hoped to avoid for themselves. Carla Long, a middle-class, American-born black wife, said, "My mother's a grudge holder. I don't want to be like that." Her parents had separated. One of the things she liked best in her own marriage was "laughing about things" together.

Extended family members were often a non-issue for African and Caribbean couples, at least on a day-to-day basis, because their families had remained behind in their home countries. Some husbands and wives mentioned being relieved that they could avoid conflict with their or their spouse's parents by living so far away, even though they also sometimes missed having the resources extended family could provide. Contact with overseas family was generally voluntary and by computer or phone, so conflict with them or about them could easily be pushed to the side. On the other hand, Caribbean wives in particular remained attached to other women in their families, sometimes visiting for months at a time with their children and without their husbands, though no Caribbean husband remarked on this as problematic.

For American-born couples, both black and white, extended families could be a source of support, providing babysitting, a shoulder to cry on, or even money, but involvement with extended family often came with a heavy emotional price that couples weren't willing to pay. Many couples complained of differences with their own parents, each other's parents, siblings—even cousins, aunts, uncles, and more distant relatives. As with Roman and Ashley, it was common for at least one in-law to dislike a spouse. Keisha Parrish's family didn't like Charles' cheating ways. Lynne Brown said of Will's family,

> I try not to say anything to his family because, you know, his mom I don't care for. She's lied on me. His dad, I don't care for … the youngest [brother]. His family's a little weird, you know? His grandmother, if one don't like you they all don't like you, basically. That's how they rumble.

Some American-born couples saw family members on a regular basis, as most had grown up near where they were currently living. Though American-born working-class and lower-income couples were some-times more dependent on family for resources such as childcare, even this was not universal, with some working-class children attending daycare and some middle-class children cared for by a family member. Closeness to family and the amount of interaction expected seemed to be based more on individual preferences and expectations than anything related to race or class. When a spouse's parents or other family members didn't approve of their marriage, the spouse tended to spend less time with those family members. Though the rejected husband or wife often felt hurt, their spouse was usually a source of comfort. It may be that couples in which a husband or wife sided with their family of origin over a spouse had split up before reaching their five-year anniversary, and thus we did not see such couples. Ultimately, conflict with outside family members, while common, did not generate significant conflict between husbands and wives in our study—if anything, it seemed to bring them closer together. As Roman began, "Yeah, it's one of those ones like her parents say something or my parents can say something …" and Ashley finished, "I'm going to defend him regardless … We're like, it's us against them."

Personal Habits and Cultural Conflict
Sometimes husbands and wives just get on each other's nerves. Barry Adams, a lower-class, American-born black husband, can't stand the

shrillness of his wife's voice when she's mad at their kids. Pamela Taylor, a white middle-class wife, doesn't like the way her husband folds the laundry. Almost every husband and wife could point to something mundane about their spouse that bothered them. When other aspects of the relationship were going well, these things were easy enough to ignore.

Among couples with an immigrant spouse and an American-born spouse, what came up more frequently, and with more consequence, was the idea of cultural conflict. Bruce Everett, a working-class, American-born black husband, doesn't like to eat possum, something his Caribbean wife thinks is an ordinary food. Emily McAvoy, a middle-class white wife, disagrees with her African husband about causes of illness and how to treat it, though she will sometimes give in and use the herbs he wants her to rub on herself in the shower when she is sick. Abeni Sesay—the American-born black wife who was looking forward to the arrival of her stepsons—thought there was a "communication barrier" in her marriage. Travon is originally from Cameroon, where English is commonly spoken, but over time Abeni realized that Travon was still struggling with American English. Since his language skills have improved, she said, "he has opened up like a flower." She admitted that before she understood the problem, she would often get angry, but since then they have begun to "talk more," which of course further improves his ability to communicate.

Many spouses in these mixed-status relationships described what two people from the same background might have viewed as a personal issue as something cultural instead. Dre Jamme, a working-class husband from Ghana married to Brianna, who is American-born black, said, "I would say it be much easier for a couple, same culture. Where they don't have to deal with different values, like religion, holidays to celebrate, or even food. It would be much easier." But, of course, marriage could be a struggle for any couple, whether their backgrounds were similar or not. And even if couples were from the same country, they could have different values, religions, or food preferences. Thinking about differences as cultural rather than personal sometimes helped couples navigate their differences more peacefully.

Making Marriages Healthy

Our couples had all been married at least five years, and some for much longer. Some had also been together for many years before they tied the knot. As such, even though research says couples' conflict style remains consistent, most of our couples reported that they had made progress in managing conflict since their relationships began. A sense of progress almost always meant that couples engaged in less destructive behaviors such as yelling, hurling insults, or even hurling objects. The Healthy Marriage Initiative was on to something in promoting communication as a key to marriage. Some couples had gradually grown to employ constructive approaches, and almost all spouses—even those that weren't getting along—talked about communication as key to resolving conflicts and being happier. Ashley believed that the best thing about her marriage to Roman was their "open communication." She said, "The more we talk, the more it brings us closer together." Makayla Scott, a working-class African wife, said that to have an ideal marriage, "regular communication is the key." Sandra Craft, a middle-class Caribbean wife, said that being willing to engage in conflict—rather than withdrawing—improved communication and the marriage. Initially, she tried to be on her "best behavior" and to do her "duty" as a biblically submissive wife. She held back and didn't argue about anything but ultimately found this to be "dysfunctional." Now she said, "I will argue," and as a result is happier in her marriage and sees herself and her husband as a "good wife" and a "good husband." Brandon Helmy, a working-class, American-born black husband, described the early years of his marriage to Tonya, also American-born black, as "on a scale from one to ten, about a four." Tonya affirmed that the early years were "kind of hard." Both attributed success in their marriage over time to their abilities to respect one another and accept each other's decisions. Brandon explained that Tonya now allows him to say that he is sorry as opposed to "her telling me that I am sorry." The two learned to keep communication open as a means to avoid polarization. Brandon said the relationships was now "an eight or nine."

Some couples found communicating harder as their marriages went on because work, children, increased responsibilities, and money troubles took so much time and also created more situations to argue about.

Alexis Addy, a middle-class African wife, said that an ideal marriage is based on "communication, laughter, happiness." The Addys described their marriage as a contrast between Alexis' free-spirited, easy-going personality and Sean's inability to compromise. Alexis said that this often caused conflict because it prevented the couple from enjoying social activities together. Sean discussed the struggle marriage presented for him, saying,

> [trying] to align my life with somebody else's is the hardest. You do things on your own if you're single, but in marriage it's different, and working together as a unit is not always that easy. I feel it's difficult a lot of the time, because we argue over things we're not supposed to argue about, because everybody is stressed and in their own little world.

To improve their marriage, Alexis wanted "more interaction, and more communication, more lovey-dovey." They weren't there yet, but they were still together and still working on it.

Other couples, rather than establishing better communication, had fewer conflicts because one or both of the spouses withdrew. Things were quieter if a spouse didn't fight back, and quieter still if neither spouse engaged in an argument. Many couples described throughout this chapter took this approach. Diamond Varner paid all the bills and stopped having sex with Eric instead of confronting him about his spending all of his income on himself. Whenever he sensed a fight brewing, Eric left the house to have "me time." In order to avoid Lynne's wrath, Will Brown gave in to her demands to tell her where he was going or to buy things for their daughters. Ron Washington retreated into the arms of other women instead of suggesting that he and Aretha attend counseling to address the imbalance in their sexual desires. Aretha ignored the problem altogether. Withdrawing from problems didn't resolve them. In some cases, it made them worse. But on a day-to-day basis, it kept the peace.

Allen and Olson describe the five types of African-American marriage, in descending order of health, as Vitalized, Harmonious, Traditional, Conflicted, and Devitalized. But they note that the type and number of conflicts they observed among their sample of several hundred black couples, as well as the distribution of types of marriages, were similar to those observed among an even larger sample of white couples.[28] Similarly, in our much smaller sample, we did not observe any group overall, whether by race, gender, country of origin, or social class, stand out in terms of happiness and satisfaction or to exhibit observable trends toward having more or less conflict. Rather, we saw certain topics that were more or less likely to generate conflict among certain groups—and this is where a one-size-fits-all approach to promoting healthy marriage may be missing the mark. Wives were far more likely than husbands to feel unfairly treated in the burdens they bore for household labor and childrearing. Everyone fought about money, but lower-income couples were more stressed than middle-class couples about having stable employment and enough money to pay for necessities—they faced many more conflicts that were outside of individual control, something that marriage education and counseling cannot remedy. Middle-class couples were more likely to accumulate debt through frivolous spending—often spending instigated by only one spouse. Stepchildren provoked conflict among white couples but very little among black couples—though the reasons for the lack of conflict appeared different among the American-born, Africans, and Caribbeans. Couples with an immigrant and an American-born spouse had cultural conflicts that ranged from religion to food—though sometimes couples from the same background had similar conflicts. Conflicts regarding sex could affect anyone, and affairs were problematic, even for wives from countries where men's extramarital relations were accepted.

Marriages operated best when each member of the couple fully invested and tried to meet the other spouse's needs, whatever those might be. When a spouse withdrew or continued to approach conflict destructively, the relationship suffered. One person could not be constructive alone—a healthy marriage was something couples had to create together. And it was hard. As Taylor McCoy said, "Marriage is a job. It takes work. And a lot of times you've got to put in overtime if you want to keep it working." Couples who fully invested in one another, putting effort into improving the relationship and being generous with each other, often described the close friendship that developed as their marriage progressed. Ashley told us that the best thing about being married was "having that person there all the time and being friends." Roman added, "For me, your spouse is supposed to be your best friend." When couples felt their marriages were healthy, they found the relationship deeply meaningful and satisfying. Many indicated they felt as Marvin Johnson, a working-class, American-born black husband, did when he told us, "Just like anything else in life, marriage has its good days and bad days, but I wouldn't trade being married to Jennifer and raising a family together for anything in the world."

Notes

1 White, James M., and David M. Klein. 2008. *Family Theories*. Los Angeles, CA: SAGE.
2 Crohan, Susan E. 1996. "Marital Quality and Conflict across the Transition to Parenthood in African American and White Couples." *Journal of Marriage and the Family* 58(4):933–944; Kurdek, Lawrence A. 1995. "Predicting Change in Marital Satisfaction from Husbands and Wives Conflict Resolution Styles." *Journal of Marriage and the Family* 57(1):153–164.
3 Birditt, Kira S., Edna Brown, Terri L. Orbuch, and Jessica M. Mcilvane. 2010. "Marital Conflict Behaviors and Implications for Divorce Over 16 Years." *Journal of Marriage and Family* 72(5):1188–1204.
4 Lyngstad, Torkild, and Marika Jalovaara. 2010. "A Review of the Antecedents of Union Dissolution." *Demographic Research* 23:257; Sweeney, Megan M., and Julie A. Phillips. 2004. "Understanding Racial Differences in Marital Disruption: Recent Trends and Explanations." *Journal of Marriage and Family* 66(3):639–650.
5 Oggins, Jean. 2003. "Topics of Marital Disagreement among African-American and Euro-American Newlyweds." *Psychological Reports* 92(2), 419–425; Papp, Lauren M., E. Mark Cummings, and Marcie C. Goeke-Morey. 2009. "For Richer, for Poorer: Money as a Topic of Marital Conflict in the Home." *Family Relations* 58(1):91–103.
6 U.S. Department of Health & Human Services. 2016. "What is HMI?" *Office of Family Assistance, ACF*. Retrieved September 12, 2017 (https://archive.acf.hhs.gov/healthymarriage/about/mission.html#background).
7 U.S. Department of Health & Human Services. 2016. "Healthy Marriage & Responsible Fatherhood." *Office of Family Assistance, ACF*. Retrieved September 12, 2017 (https://www.acf.hhs.gov/ofa/programs/healthy-marriage).
8 U.S. Department of Health & Human Services, 2016.
9 Institute for American Values. 2011. "Why Marriage Matters: Thirty Conclusions from the Social Sciences." *Center for Marriage and Families at the Institute for American Values*. Retrieved September 12, 2017 (www.americanvalues.org).
10 Ribar, David C. 2015. "Why Marriage Matters for Child Wellbeing." *The Future of Children* 25(2):11–27.
11 Cummings, E. Mark, Marcie C. Goeke-Morey, and Lauren M. Papp. 2016. "Couple Conflict, Children, and Families: It's Not Just You and Me, Babe." Pp. 117–148 in *Couples in Conflict: Classic Edition*, edited by A. Booth, A. C. Crouter, and M. Clements. New York: Routledge.
12 Amato, Paul R. 2010. "Research on Divorce: Continuing Trends and New Developments." *Journal of Marriage and Family* 72(3):650–666.

13 U.S. Department of Health & Human Services, 2016.

14 The Gottman Institute. n.d. "Research." *The Gottman Institute*. Retrieved September 12, 2017 (https://www.gottman.com/about/research/).

15 Johnson, Matthew D. 2012. "Healthy Marriage Initiatives: On the Need for Empiricism in Policy Implementation." *American Psychologist* 67(4):296–308.

16 Stack, Carol B. 1975. *All Our Kin: Strategies for Survival in a Black Community*. New York: Basic Books; Taylor, Robert Joseph, Linda M. Chatters, Amanda Toler Woodward, and Edna Brown. 2013. "Racial and Ethnic Differences in Extended Family, Friendship, Fictive Kin, and Congregational Informal Support Networks." *Family Relations* 62(4):609–624.

17 Fomby, Paula, and Andrew J. Cherlin. 2007. "Family Instability and Child Well-Being." *American Sociological Review* 72(2):181–204.

18 Whisman, Mark A., Kristina Coop Gordon, and Yael Chatav. 2007. "Predicting Sexual Infidelity in a Population-Based Sample of Married Individuals." *Journal of Family Psychology* 21(2):320–324.

19 Martin, Rachel. 2015. "Sorting Through the Numbers on Infidelity." *NPR*. Retrieved September 12, 2017 (http://www.npr.org/2015/07/26/426434619/sorting-through-the-numbers-on-infidelity); Munsch, Christin L. 2012. "The Science of Two-Timing: The State of Infidelity Research." *Sociology Compass* 6(1):46–59.

20 Whisman, Mark A., and Douglas K. Snyder. 2007. "Sexual Infidelity in a National Survey of American Women: Differences in Prevalence and Correlates as a Function of Method of Assessment." *Journal of Family Psychology* 21(2):147–154.

21 Collins, Patricia. H. 2004. *Black Sexual Politics: African Americans, Gender, and the New Racism*. New York: Routledge.

22 Anderson, Patricia, and Camille Daley. 2015. "African-Caribbean Fathers: The Conflict between Masculinity and Fathering." Pp. 13–38 in *Fathers Across Cultures: The Importance, Roles, and Diverse Practices of Dads*, edited by J. Roopnarine. Santa Barbara, CA: ABC-CLIO.

23 Fenske, James. 2015. "African Polygamy: Past and Present." *Journal of Development Economics* 117:58–73.

24 Blow, Adrian J., and Kelley Hartnett. 2005. "Infidelity in Committed Relationships II: A Substantive Review." *Journal of Marital and Family Therapy* 31(2):217–233.

25 Moore, Kristin A., Susan Jekielek, Jacinta Bronte-Tinkew, Lina Guzman, Suzanne Ryan, and Zakia Redd. 2004. "What is 'Healthy Marriage?' Defining the Concept." *Child Trends Research Brief* 16:1–8.

26 Previti, Denise, and Paul R. Amato. (2004). "Is Infidelity a Cause or a Consequence of Poor Marital Quality?" *Journal of Social and Personal Relationships* 21(2):217–230.

27 Rhode, Deborah L. 2016. *Adultery*. Cambridge, MA: Harvard University Press.

28 Allen, William D., and David H. Olson. 2001. "Five Types of African-American Marriages." *Journal of Marital and Family Therapy* 27(3):301–314.

8

A NEW LENS ON BLACK MARRIAGE

There are many lenses for viewing the world. If we choose the same lens over and over, we see what we already know and reaffirm established perceptions. A single lens can become like the proverbial hammer that makes everything look like a nail. Marriage is complicated, and when scholars, therapists, and journalists view black couples through the lens of deficiency, it isn't hard to find problems. The problems become proof that black marriages are unhealthy, unsuccessful, or almost nonexistent, and the justification for a deficiency lens is renewed.

This book is not designed to deflect from problems faced by black couples in America. It is true that fewer black Americans than those of other races and ethnicities are marrying, and given the social and political privileges married people enjoy, this can be to their disadvantage. Instead, this research sought to tell the stories of young, contemporary black couples who *did* marry. The research for this book tested a new lens, one that asks: Who is part of the Millennial generation of black married couples in America? What makes black couples choose to marry? How do black married couples reach their fifth (or eighth or thirteenth) anniversary, and what does it look like when they get there? If we consider being married at least five years as marital success, what does that lens reveal that is different from what we see when we look at couples who divorce or who never marry at all?

Marriage's Place in the Life Course

Marriage is not as important to most Americans as it once was. Cohabitation has entered adulthood's path as an ordinary stepping-stone.[1] The term "spinster" for an unmarried woman—once a term of derision and pity—is almost never applied in the modern day. Advances in contraception have made it possible to have heterosexual intercourse with a much lower risk of pregnancy. Sex outside of marriage carries little stigma except among the most religious—and even very religious people who view premarital sex as sinful usually do it anyway. Most women and men become sexually active in late adolescence and have multiple sex partners before beginning to consider marriage.[2] If an unmarried woman does get pregnant, she can decide to have the baby and raise it whether she marries or not. The average age for women's first births is now younger than the average age for their first marriages.[3] Gone are the days of universal social shaming or forcing unmarried women to give their babies up for adoption.[4] Gone, also, are the days of the "shotgun wedding": more than 40% of American children are born to unmarried mothers, with rates among black women about twice that of white women,[5] and a conception outside of marriage rarely results in a wedding before the birth anymore.[6] Before the 1970s, fathers had no rights when it came to children born outside of marriage—and mothers had no rights to make financial or social demands on them. Now there are legal and social obligations and opportunities for fathers, whether they are married to their child's mother or not.[7] Marriage is much more fragile than parenthood—it's considerably more difficult (and much less common) to terminate parental rights than it is to get a divorce.

Despite these revolutionary changes, Americans as a whole remain more committed to marriage as an institution than many of their counterparts in other industrialized nations.[8] Part of the reason gay and lesbian Americans fought so hard for the right to marry in the United States is that both legal and social benefits of marriage remain high relative to being—or being perceived as—a cohabiting or single adult.[9] American blacks are part of that ongoing trend. Even though black Americans are less likely to marry than their counterparts of other races and ethnicities, over the course of their lives, the majority do still marry,[10] and the majority of black Americans say that when couples plan to spend the rest of their lives together, it is "very important" that they marry.[11]

Life course theory asserts there is a series of steps that individuals go through on their path through adulthood. Generally, while some of the steps may begin with a single event (e.g. a courthouse wedding), the step impacts the person for a long time (e.g. a marriage). Under this theoretical umbrella, most believe there is a "best" way to navigate the stepping stones on life's path. But the best course is not fixed. Just as a road map changes over time as new subdivisions develop, old bridges are rebuilt, or freeways reshape the most efficient way to get from here to there, life's most traveled paths change with an evolving society. Social movements, social policies, economic shifts, political turnover, globalization, and more affect American individuals and families, and thus help to determine paths of the life course. This is what life course theorists call "the contextual challenge."[12]

An American's age when he or she first marries is the latest ever recorded. During the 1950s and '60s, age at first marriage was the lowest since the Census began keeping records, hovering around age 20 for women and 22 or 23 for men. By the late 1990s and early 2000s, when all of our couples married, the median age was around 25 for women and 26 or 27 for men. And it has continued to go up since, surpassing any point in the past, reaching 27 or 28 for women and 29 or 30 for men by 2016.[13] Age at first marriage is higher the more education a person has, but it is also higher for blacks than it is for whites.[14] Coupled with these trends is, by default, a lower proportion of adults who are married—about half of all adults in 2010 (when we completed our interviews), in contrast to nearly three-quarters in the early 1970s. For blacks, the percentage is even lower—a little over a third of black men were married, and less than a third of black women.[15] But even though nearly 40% of adults surveyed said marriage is becoming obsolete, almost half of the unmarried adults who agreed with this statement still hoped to marry.[16]

What these statistics tell us is that it is now perfectly normal to be an unmarried adult. The ideal life course has changed over time. In the mid-twentieth century, couples married young and often had children right away, before becoming established in a career and buying a home. In the twenty-first century, people are more likely to use early adulthood to establish themselves in the job market and perhaps sow their wild oats. Marriage has become the capstone to establishing adulthood rather than its foundation,[17] and it's no longer regarded as a non-negotiable obligation of adult life. Our couples were bucking modern trends, as most had married in their early- to mid-twenties. Some had begun their relationships as early as middle school. But in a twist on past tradition, most had children before they married, with some beginning parenthood as early as age 14. Though in nearly a third of our couples one or both spouses had at least one child from a former partner, very few of our participants had been married to anyone other than their current spouse. And our black couples, especially those who were American-born, often felt they were bucking trends in their own communities when they decided to marry.

Race, Immigrants, and Reasons to Marry

Our white couples, especially the middle-class couples, were most likely to cling to an older version of the ideal life course. Several women mentioned having a specific timeline in mind for when marriage and childbearing should occur, ages that were far earlier than contemporary averages. As Amy Abbas told us, "I wanted to be married by a certain age … I don't know whether it's biological clockwork or just wanting to have a goal or a plan." White couples often talked about marriage as if it were obligatory. Pamela and Richard Taylor stammered when asked why they decided to marry, until Richard finally blurted, "It was either get married or it was time to break up. It just felt like it was time." Despite these findings, recent data show that while marriage rates continue to decrease for both blacks and whites, the decreases for whites are now steeper.[18] Scholars such as Robert Staples and Valora Washington have stated that blacks are the "vanguard"[19] of American family patterns in modern times, where white marital patterns have piggybacked on that of the black population. We certainly saw evidence of this among the working- and lower-class study couples in regard to their nonmarital childbearing. Thus, it is possible that white couples will increasingly release the idea of marriage being an obligation for parenthood and also as a must for long-term relational intimacy.

American-born black couples rarely spoke of marital timelines. Although a few had always planned to marry someone eventually, more often couples—especially working- and lower-class couples—said that being together for a long time and having children together had proved they were compatible. A few couples had "love at first sight" experiences. Many discussed being best friends. White couples didn't commonly identify love and deep friendship as motivations for marriage. American-born black couples did. Marriage decisions among American-born blacks were very much based on finding the right individual rather than feeling an obligation to the institution. Marlon Byrd said of his decision to marry Gwen, "When you get something good, you got to hold on to it." Even when there were social or religious reasons to marry, American-born black spouses discussed love as a motivator and marriage as deeply personal, as did Bruce Everett, who was partially—but only partially—motivated to marry by his Muslim faith:

> The best thing about marriage is the fulfillment of God's will ... Whether you have children or not; I guess [that's] optional. I think a man needs a woman, and a woman needs a man. We're like two pieces to one puzzle ... Love, it makes you stronger, it makes you much more confident, you know, it's just so much for you.

Immigrant black couples offered more of a mix of perspectives. Africans, who hailed from many countries and cultures, were likely to view marriage as a normative life stage. Among Caribbeans, some married for love; one couple mentioned marrying in response to a pregnancy. Few of our couples of any background had a church wedding. By far the most common course of action was to go to the courthouse, sometimes with a few close friends or family members, sometimes alone. Occasionally couples who married at the courthouse had a party, but more often the wedding was a quiet and private affair.

African and Caribbean spouses were often condemning of American-born blacks and their marriage patterns—especially American-born black men. Immigrants were particularly critical of infidelity, divorce, and absentee fathers, even though among Caribbeans such patterns are common, and several Caribbean husbands we interviewed had themselves abandoned children born to previous partners. Africans critical of American-born black fathers also told us that most men had little direct involvement in childrearing in their home countries and often did not treat their wives with respect. As has been found by other researchers, black immigrants sometimes went out of their way to maintain an ethnic identity and differentiate their family and social patterns from those of American-born blacks, perhaps attempting to avoid the stark racism so often directed at American-born blacks in particular.[20]

Policy, Values, and Healthy Marriage

Post-welfare-reform social policy embraced the assumption that getting married could offer a means out of poverty, but it is perhaps more likely that getting out of poverty supports healthy marriage. Stress and conflict can plague any marriage. Some couples have easygoing temperaments, and some are more high-strung. Some spouses are flexible in their behaviors, willing to learn and change and eager to work toward better communication with a partner. Couples who lash out at each other or withdraw, regardless of any other aspect of their social position, are less likely to fare well than those who learn to handle conflict constructively.

But lower-income couples, especially black couples, face structural racism and many other stressors that no marriage education program could ever alleviate. These include economic changes of the last decades that reduced the number of manufacturing jobs; wage stagnation; criminal justice policies that target black men for arrest and prosecution; job market discrimination; and a constant bombardment of negative portrayals of black families in the media. All present a constant challenge to the success of black marriages. In many of our black couples, the ones who were making it despite the odds, spouses spoke of the support they found in each other, saying the best thing about marriage was, "We're in this together," "I can talk to him about *anything*," or "I know she always has my back." Given how high divorce rates are when couples have stable housing, employment, and other resources, it is miraculous that these couples had made it through five years or more of marriage despite joblessness, jail time, housing instability, children with disabilities, or not having enough money to turn on the heat – on top of the mundane stresses of marriage and parenting. It might make more sense to further study how financially disadvantaged couples are making marriage work, rather than believing a well-meaning program can teach them how to make it work. What most of these couples needed had nothing to do with marriage education and everything to do with money, jobs, and social dignity.

As discussed earlier in this book, scholars have long posited that black marriages are more egalitarian than marriages among those of other racial–ethnic groups, particularly whites. This belief seems to have stemmed from a history of workforce participation among black women. However, the majority of black immigrants came to America in more recent years, after women's labor force participation had become more common among all groups.

So, is it true that black couples are more egalitarian overall? When we consider the full class spectrum and immigrants from the Caribbean and Africa in addition to American-born blacks, the answer isn't simple. Africans, who had usually lived separate, gendered lives in their home countries, felt adjusting to American values (which they interpreted as egalitarian values) to be an essential component of living in the United States. Many of them discovered that they liked sharing the roles of paid work and home life. Especially at home, contributions were not always exactly equal, but they were a far cry from what would have been expected in Africa. In contrast, most Caribbean spouses vocally rejected egalitarianism, claiming the husband as household head and primary breadwinner. Even when gendered role division was not working, many Caribbean couples felt an obligation to *make* it work, often citing the Bible as their guide.

Some American-born black couples also believed in a biblical mandate for male headship and wifely submission, but unexpectedly, for American-born blacks these beliefs tended to draw spousal roles closer rather than to further separate them. For a man to be a household head, he had to be involved in the family, and because of the long history of wives and mothers in the workforce among American-born blacks, American-born black women didn't see anything contradictory about being a submissive wife and also having a paid job. Despite the gendered rhetoric, these couples shared everything. Many other American-born blacks specifically believed in having egalitarian relationships, though ironically they weren't always as skilled at putting egalitarianism into effect.

Middle-class spouses were most likely among whites to believe in egalitarianism, though in all cases women still bore a heavier burden of home labor. Lower-income whites were often poorer precisely because they believed in and enacted a gendered division of labor despite being unable to make ends meet on one income. Our couples countered the arguments of economist Gary Becker that specialization is the route to a harmonious and prosperous marriage. Specializing did not make husbands earn more—it just made it harder to pay the bills. Most of our couples who came closest to shared income earning, housework, and childrearing appeared happier than those who specialized, regardless of what ideology brought them to sharing.

The End of the Beginning

This book is not the definitive story of contemporary marriage for black Americans. We interviewed sixty-one couples in one metropolitan area at one point in time. Though we had great diversity among our couples in terms of class and representation of the African diaspora, that diversity meant that we did not have a large number of individuals or couples who represented any particular intersectional identity of race, class, gender, and culture. We did not include couples in same-sex marriages, which have become legal nationally since we conducted our original interviews. Most of the couples we interviewed had computers and used the Internet, but we conducted most of our research before the explosion of social media platforms such as Instagram or Tinder and before owning a smartphone became a near-requirement of American existence.

What this book does offer is a starting point for a new lens for viewing marriage, family, and social institutions and the way they apply among contemporary black families in the United States. We find that black Americans *indeed want to marry*—and some get married, stay married, and are very happy together. Some get married and stay married but are less happy. The American black couples interviewed were committed not just to marrying but to negotiating differences, improving communication, and being there for each other as best they could. When the focus of black marriage is not marriage but non-marriage and divorce, it's impossible to see what makes marriage work. The assumption becomes that the problems that lead black couples to postpone or avoid marriage or lead married couples to have higher rates of divorce are the problems at the heart of all black marriages.

We interviewed diverse couples and found great diversity in their marriages—but not always in the ways we expected. Sometimes we saw differences among black couples by their country of origination, as we did with attitudes regarding egalitarianism. In other cases, class differences predominated, as with the high levels of stress lower-class marriages endured as couples tried to stretch an inadequate income. We saw non-marital or premarital childbearing across all lower-income couples, regardless of race, but among the middle class, we saw that whites approached childbearing within marriage as a requirement, while middle-class black couples regarded it more as a bonus. Africans tended to strive to adjust to American life, while Caribbeans were more interested in preserving values from back home. We also learned more than we anticipated from mixed marriages—those in which one spouse was American-born and the other was an immigrant. Such relationships offered a new lens on both cultures, with each member of the couple forced to see their own norms through the eyes of their partner. One thing became clear: difference is not deficiency.

If there is one takeaway that all readers gain from this book, we hope it will be that there is no such thing as "black marriage" or "the black family," any more than we would expect to apply a universal view to all white couples or white families—or couples of any race or ethnicity. Intersectional theorists have taught us that there are many identities contained within each of us, and it is this particular collection of traits in a particular societal context that determines our experiences and perceptions and frames the way others see us. That black couples are made up of women and men, of those descended from American slaves and those newly arrived from Ghana or Trinidad, of practicing dentists and those trying to eke out a few hours of day labor, of parents, stepparents, the childless, Christians, Muslims, and more is itself a statement that there is no way to categorize black marriage as a single institution. We hope this book will inspire scholars to look for new lenses to view marriage, family, and black life in America, abandoning a single line of sight and creating a rounded picture of all there is to see.

Notes

1 Kennedy, Sheela, and Catherine A. Fitch. 2012. "Measuring Cohabitation and Family Structure in the United States: Assessing the Impact of New Data from the Current Population Survey." *Demography* 49(4):1479–1498.

2 Regnerus, Mark, and Jeremy Uecker. 2011. *Premarital Sex in America: How Young Americans Meet, Mate, and Think About Marrying.* Oxford: Oxford University Press.

3 Centers for Disease Control and Prevention. 2016. "Mean Age of Mothers Is on the Rise: United States, 2000–2014." *Centers for Disease Control and Prevention.* Retrieved September 13, 2017 (https://www.cdc.gov/nchs/products/databriefs/db232.htm).

4 Fessler, Ann. 2007. *The Girls Who Went Away: The Hidden History of Women Who Surrendered Children for Adoption in the Decades before Roe v. Wade.* New York: Penguin Press.

5 Martin, Joyce A., E. Brady Hamilton, Michelle J. K. Osterman, Anne K. Driscoll, and T. J. Mathews. 2017. "Births: Final Data for 2015." *National Vital Statistics Report* 66(1).

6 Sweeney, Megan M., and R. Kelly Raley. 2014. "Race, Ethnicity, and the Changing Context of Childbearing in the United States." *Annual Review of Sociology* 40(1):539–558.

7 Child Welfare Information Gateway. 2014. *The Rights of Unmarried Fathers.* Washington, D.C.: U.S. Department of Health and Human Services, Children's Bureau. Retrieved September 13, 2017 (https://www.childwelfare.gov/pubPDFs/putative.pdf).

8 Cherlin, Andrew J. 2004. "The Deinstitutionalization of American Marriage." *Journal of Marriage and Family* 66(4):848–861.

9 Brandzel, Amy L. 2005. "Queering Citizenship? Same-Sex Marriage and the State." *GLQ: A Journal of Lesbian and Gay Studies* 11(2):171–204.

10 Raley, R. Kelly, Megan M. Sweeney, and Danielle Wondra. 2015. "The Growing Racial and Ethnic Divide in US Marriage Patterns." *The Future of Children/Center for the Future of Children, the David and Lucile Packard Foundation* 25(2):89–109.

11 Wang, Wendy, and Kim Parker. 2014. "Record Share of Americans Have Never Married: As Values, Economics and Gender Patterns Change." *Pew Research Center.* Retrieved September 12, 2017 (http://www.pewsocialtrends.org/2014/09/24/record-share-of-americans-have-never-married/).

12 Elder, Glen H. Jr., Monica Kirkpatrick Johnson, and Robert Crosnoe. 2003. "The Emergence and Development of Life Course Theory." Pp. 3–19 in *Handbook of the Life Course,* edited by J. T. Mortimer and M. J. Shanahan. New York: Springer US.

13 U.S. Bureau of the Census. 2016. "Table MS–2: Estimated Median Age at First Marriage, by Sex: 1890 to the Present." *Historical Marital Status Tables.* Retrieved September 13, 2017 (https://www.census.gov/data/tables/time-series/demo/families/marital.html).

14 Aughinbaugh, Alison, Omar Robles, and Hugette Sun. 2013. "Marriage and Divorce: Patterns by Gender, Race, and Educational Attainment." *Monthly Labor Review.* U.S. Bureau of Labor Statistics. Retrieved September 13, 2017 (https://www.bls.gov/opub/mlr/2013/article/marriage-and-divorce-patterns-by-gender-race-and-educational-attainment.htm); Raley et al., 2015.

15 U.S. Bureau of the Census. 2016. "MS–1. Marital Status of the Population 15 Years Old and Over by Sex, Race and Hispanic Origin: 1950 to Present." *Historical Marital Status*

Tables. Retrieved September 13, 2017 (https://www.census.gov/data/tables/time-series/demo/families/marital.html).

16　Wang and Parker, 2014.

17　Edin, Kathryn, and Maria Kefalas. 2011. *Promises I Can Keep: Why Poor Women Put Motherhood Before Marriage*. Berkeley: University of California Press; Rosenfeld, Michael J. 2009. *The Age of Independence: Interracial Unions, Same-Sex Unions, and the Changing American Family*. Cambridge: Harvard University Press.

18　Cohn, D'Vera, Jeffrey S. Passel, Wendy Wang, and Gretchen Livingston. 2011. "Appendix: Additional Tables." *Pew Research Center*. Retrieved September 13, 2017 (http://www.pewsocialtrends.org/2011/12/14/appendix-additional-tables/).

19　Staples, Robert. 1999. "Sociocultural Factors in Black Family Transformation: Toward Redefinition of Family Functions." Pp.18–23 in *The Black Family: Essays and Studies*, 6th ed. Belmont, CA: Wadsworth Publishing Co.; Washington, Valora. 1988. "The Black Mother in the United States." Pp. 185–213 in *The Different Faces of Motherhood*, edited by Beverly Birns and Dale F. Hay. New York: Springer.

20　Smith, Candis W. 2014. *Black Mosaic: The Politics of Black Pan-Ethnic Diversity*. New York: New York University Press; Waters, Mary C. 2009. *Black Identities: West Indian Immigrant Dreams and American Realities*. Cambridge: Harvard University Press.

APPENDIX A

THE STUDY COUPLES

Name	Ethnicity (wife/husband)	Social Class Designation
Abbas, Amy & Muhammed	White/Central Asian	Middle
Adams, Christine & Barry	American-born	Lower
Addy, Alexis & Sean	African	Middle
Albright, Thandi & Lamar	Caribbean	Middle
Alderson, Clarissa & Sonny	American-born	Working
Barlow, Ashley & Roman	American-born	Middle
Brown, Lynne & William	White	Lower
Buckley, Tracy & Kenneth	African	Middle
Byrd, Gwen & Marlon	American-born	Working
Chebet, Alena & Danny	African	Middle
Craft, Sandra & Donald	Caribbean/American-born	Middle
Crawford, Lily & Patrick	American-born	Working
Davis, James & Mia	Caribbean	Working
Dawit, Hannah & Emmanuel	American-born/African	Middle
Erickson, Kristina & Franklin	American-born	Middle
Everett, Francoise & Bruce	Caribbean/American-born	Working
Gardner, Netra & Adam	American-born	Working
Glasser, Destiny & Terrell	American-born	Middle
Goodman, Kalinda & Simeon	African	Middle
Greene, Melanie & Michael	White	Working
Helmy, Tonya & Brandon	American-born	Working

(Continued)

Name	Ethnicity (wife/husband)	Social Class Designation
Holmes, Kelly & Hank	American-born/Caribbean	Middle
Johnson, Jennifer & Marvin	American-born	Middle
Jones, Donna & Joshua	White	Lower
Kelly, Charlene & Albert	American-born	Middle
Kennedy, Meredith & Allen	White	Middle
Koffi, Mekelle & Kingston	African	Lower
Larson, Erin & Alex	White	Working
Lewis, Jasmine & Jackson	American-born/Caribbean	Middle
Long, Carla & Quin	American-born	Middle
Martin, Ruth & Elijah	American-born	Working
McAllister, Lori & Bart	American-born	Lower
McAvoy, Emily & Jacob	White/African	Middle
McCoy, Taylor & Gabriel	Caribbean	Working
Morrison, Edwina & Rashid	American-born/Caribbean	Working
Naki, Sophia & Daniel	American-born/African	Working
Palmer, Mary Ann & Joe	White	Lower
Parish, Keisha & Charles	American-born	Working
Peterson, Morgan & Landon	Caribbean	Middle
Posner, Karen & Ted	White	Lower
Powell, Sue Ann & Jeff	White	Lower
Rowe, Mariah & Jonathan	American-born	Lower
Russell, Sharon & David	American-born	Lower
Ryan, Shenice & Dixon	Caribbean/American-born	Working
Scott, Makayla & Isaiah	African	Working
Sesay, Abeni & Travon	American-born/African	Working
Sheldon, Mercedes & Montel	Caribbean	Middle
Smith, Denise & Emmett	American-born	Middle
Spencer, Melea & Booker	American-born/African	Working
Springfield, Candy & Ethan	White	Working
Taylor, Pamela & Richard	White	Middle
Thompson, Laura & Mike	White	Lower
Tompkins, Ava & Anthony	Caribbean/American-born	Middle
Trotter, Samantha & Ryan	Caribbean/American-born	Middle
Varner, Diamond & Eric	American-born	Working
Velarde, Kylie & Odell	Caribbean	Working
Waller, Michelle & Andrew	White	Middle
Washington, Aretha & Ron	American-born	Middle
Wilcox, Bethany & Harold	White	Working
Yabu, Joyce & Rahim	American-born/African	Working

APPENDIX B

CONTEMPORARY BLACK MARRIAGE STUDY RESEARCH METHODOLOGY

In pursuing a paradigm shift in our approach to research on the African-American family, we triangulated multiple methods to interpret the subjective experience of black marriage. Our goal was to look broadly and in-depth at contemporary black married life, and to present black married couples with an empowering narrative as opposed to constant examinations of family dysfunction commonly fixated upon by social scientists, policymakers, and the media. Our approach is best understood as a mix of narrative and phenomenological strategy. We sought to bring both the experiences of these couples and the subjective meanings of these experiences to the center of marriage discourse. We consciously and actively worked to unpack blackness across Black classes and cultures to unlatch the analyses of black people's lives from a constricted, monolithic frame. We insist that black marriages, like black people themselves, must be understood from their specific historical, social, and cultural influences. Our aim was to reveal both shared and distinct aspects of values and married life.

Marriage in Black combines in-depth interviews with husbands and wives as couples and as individual spouses; family-based observational data; Internet marriage diaries compiled by some husbands and wives for several months after the interviews; and marriage assessments measured via a brief validated survey instrument. As John Creswell explains, those of us who employ qualitative methods for our sociological work do because we seek complexity over quantification and detail over generalized tendencies.[1] He argues that our success with this rests on "talking directly with people, going to their homes or places of work, and allowing them to tell the stories unencumbered by what we expect to find or what we have read in the literature" (40). He also believes that operating from a democratic mindset helps to attenuate the power dynamics between researcher and study participant.

To learn about young, contemporary black marriages in all their diversity—and how these marriages compare to those of similarly situated whites—we sought out couples in their thirties who had been married for at least five years. It is common in social research to mark marital survival in five-year stages once the five-year mark is obtained.[2] Though it is true that many marriages do ultimately fail among all racial–ethnic groups, even after the first five years when the divorce rate is steepest, rarely do we note that about 50% of black marriages *survive* for twenty straight years or longer. In order to capture initial levels of marital commitment and stability, we chose to meet with black couples who had been married for at least five years, though many had been married much longer.

Because we also wanted to capture contemporary attitudes and marital practices, we chose in 2007 to focus on couples who were born after the great social and legal shifts that came with the Civil Rights and Second-Wave Feminist Movements (born approximately between 1968 and 1980). That is, for all of our couples, at least one spouse had to be between the ages of 30 and 39. We sought information about how black couples in contemporary times manage to marry and maintain their marriages despite many obstacles, from the high incarceration rates of black men, to the decline in living wage jobs and the financial fluctuations of the housing market, to the lack of social supports for families with young children. These are adults who either are, or are on the cusp between, Generation X and Millennials.

To meet these couples, we began with a database from a previous study of school children conducted by Karl Alexander and Doris Entwisle, colleagues of ours at Johns Hopkins University. All of their participants were of the same age and had reached their early thirties when we began our work. The participants had been intentionally selected to represent blacks and whites from a broad social class spectrum. We contacted all black participants who were currently married and had been married at least five years, recruiting twenty of the original African-American participants along with an additional fourteen white participants to serve as a comparison.

Because we were particularly interested in diversity in the black population, we further sought married couples in which one or both spouses were black and had been born in an African or Caribbean country. We went on to recruit an additional fourteen couples in which at least one spouse had immigrated from the Caribbean and another thirteen in which at least one spouse had immigrated from Africa. These couples also had to have been married at least five years and at least one spouse had to be aged 30 to 39. Recruiting these couples was more challenging than expected, but we ultimately obtained a sample by posting signs in ethnic businesses and around universities, passing out flyers at local ethnic festivals, speaking to taxi drivers and other community employees, contacting local organizations that served refugees or other immigrants, and (most successfully) posting regular solicitations on a local Craigslist site.

We ultimately interviewed sixty-one couples, meeting with each couple at a location of their choice, which was almost always their home. The couples were divided by convenience among the two researchers, one American-born black and one white, who conducted all interviews and made all of the observations for this study. Only one couple we contacted requested a race-matched interviewer, and this couple (both spouses were American-born black) ultimately decided not to participate in the study. At times, a graduate or undergraduate research assistant accompanied the researcher to assist and contributed his or her own field notes. After introductions were made and the signing of consent forms completed, the researcher had the husband and wife fill out separate surveys about their marital satisfaction (see Appendix C). The couple was then interviewed for about one to two hours. They were asked to tell the story of how they met and how they decided to get married. They were also asked to talk about other married couples they know (as points of comparison), about what they believe makes for an "ideal" marriage, and how close they felt they were to meeting their ideals. They talked about their children, born of their union or not, and before or after the marriage. They discussed what daily married life is like between them and what they felt were the best and worst things about being married. The couples were asked to express how social factors, such as changes in women's education and workforce participation and the increase in incarceration among black men, had affected black marriage. And because we were terribly intrigued by a 2006 *Washington Post* article[3] that quoted adolescent African Americans saying that "marriage is for white people," we asked the couples to react to the comment in light of what they had experienced in marriage and among black families in their environment.

Some interviews were raucous, with multiple children darting in and out of the interview space. The interviews were often punctuated with the father pulling his son off the mantelpiece or the mother changing a baby's diaper. It was not uncommon for small children to crawl over our laps and start babbling into our recording devices. Small children put stickers on our arms and showed us their Lego collections. Other interviews were much quieter, with couples who took time to warm up, approaching the initial questions with caution. Some couples gave tours of their homes or proudly displayed their wedding albums; others remained planted on the living room couch. By the end of the interview, however, virtually every spouse was talking over his or her partner, intent on telling a preferred version of stories, laughing, chiming in with details, correcting facts—and sometimes quarrelling.

After interviewing the couple together, we spoke to each spouse separately and isolated from the other spouse, sometimes on the same day or a few days later. We made clear that the purpose of the individual interview was not to encourage the one spouse to "tell on" the other, but rather to give each spouse a chance to expand on the issues addressed in the couple interview (though spouses often did take this opportunity to "tell it like it really is"). Sometimes they revealed addictions, affairs, or the desire to separate from their spouse. Some spouses revealed dissatisfaction with their marriages and made comparisons between their current relationships and those they had with others in the past. Sometimes we witnessed individual interactions with children during these interviews that contradicted a couple's narrative of shared parenting and marital equality—or of starkly differentiated roles. Many individual interviews lasted about a half hour and revealed little new information, but some went on as long as the couple interview or even longer.

We joined most couples for a family activity, often a meal or playtime with children, allowing up to an hour for us to observe their interactions with each other. Ten couples also chose to keep Internet diaries for up to six months after the interviews. We received over 250 diary entries in all, some revealing the evolution or resolution of marital conflicts over time. Some spouses exposed further secrets in these entries as well—a husband resumed using cocaine, a wife lamented her husband's infidelities, and a father revealed his hostility toward his stepdaughter, for example.

Interviews were transcribed by research assistants, professional transcribers, and us. The validated survey data was also compiled and analyzed, but revealed little, as the results showed a general regression toward the mean, with little variation among couples or between husbands and wives. We thus focused on the richness of the data from interviews, observations, and internet diaries. We coded data using both closed and open codes. Data was compiled into a profile for each couple that was based on the framework of the interview guide and included salient details from all three interviews and from field notes. Profiles focused on the couple's ideal view of marriage; the couple's sense of what marriage is like generally; the couple's view of what *their* marriage is like; how the couple gets along regarding money, sex, children, employment, their division of labor, and interactions with friends and extended family; and anything salient they said regarding race, ethnicity, or religion. Subsequently, we reviewed all transcripts for other salient themes, using a grounded theory approach, and entered both open and closed coding into MAXQDA, a qualitative data analysis software package. Continuing with an iterative approach, we developed the most prominent and meaningful themes into book chapters that considered the intersectionality of couples' identities as well as the most salient themes that emerged in the analysis.

Our analysis employs a marital life course perspective, allowing the reader to follow the process by which the couples met each other, decided that they wanted to be married to one another, and then set out to make marital life work. The analysis also addresses the importance of class and ethnic culture in considerations of black marriage in the United States. We seek to understand how definitions and experiences of marriage differ among culturally distinct black groups in order to enhance a general body of knowledge regarding black marriage and marriage in general and to help guide public policy and social interventions in ways appropriate for all couples. We accomplished this through an inductive analytic approach,[4] where we allowed theories, hypotheses, concepts, and themes to emerge from engaging intensely with the data. We sought to identify patterns of beliefs, practices, reasoning, sentiments, and articulations within and among the study couples. This required months of repeated reading of transcripts, listening to audio files, and data coding.[5] Our research methodology data analysis plan was approved by the Institutional Review Board at Johns Hopkins University.

Notes

1   Creswell, John. 2002. *Research Design: Qualitative, Quantitative, and Mixed Method Approaches.* Thousand Oaks, CA: Sage Publications.
2   See, for example, Raley, R. Kelly, and Larry Bumpass. 2003. "The Topography of the Divorce Plateau: Levels and Trends in Union Stability in the United States after 1980." *Demographic Research* 8:245–260; and Copen, Casey E., Kimberly Daniels, Jonathan Vespa, and William D. Mosher. 2012. "First Marriages in the United States: Data from the 2006–2010 National Survey of Family Growth." *National Health Statistics Reports* 49. Hyattsville, MD: Centers for Disease Control and Prevention National Center for Health Statistics. Retrieved December 2, 2017 (https://www.cdc.gov/nchs/data/nhsr/nhsr049.pdf).
3   Jones, Joy. 2006. "'Marriage Is for White People'." *Washington Post*, March 30. Retrieved May 27, 2007 (http://www.washingtonpost.com/ wp-dyn/content/article/2006/03/25/ AR2006032500029.html).
4   See Thomas, David R. 2006. "A General Inductive Approach for Analyzing Qualitative Evaluation Data." *American Journal of Evaluation* 27:237–246.
5   See Ryan, Gery W., and H. Russell Bernard. 2003. "Techniques to Identify Themes." *Field Methods* 15:85–109.

APPENDIX C

INTERVIEW FIELD GUIDE: THE CONTEMPORARY BLACK MARRIAGE STUDY

PRINCIPAL INVESTIGATORS: KATRINA BELL McDONALD AND CAITLIN CROSS-BARNET

Directions: The couple and individual spouse interviews are intended to be only mildly structured to allow for a free-flowing conversation among the parties. The following items highlight the kind of subject matter we want to be sure to collect over the course of the conversation. Basic demographic and other background information will have already been collected via the survey instrument; this information should be consulted as necessary during the conversation. We must be mindful to use conversational language that is appropriate for the couple at hand.

Each husband and wife will be asked to cover this same terrain again separately, in private when no one else is home or with the spouse. Explain the separate interview is intended to allow that spouse to clarify or expand on what was said in the couple interview or go in a different direction altogether. This is an opportunity to probe more deeply into ethnic, gender, and class issues.

Pay close attention throughout the interview to references to marital/family "headship" and racial/ethnic-specific content. When it is appropriate, interject into the conversation questions about headship.

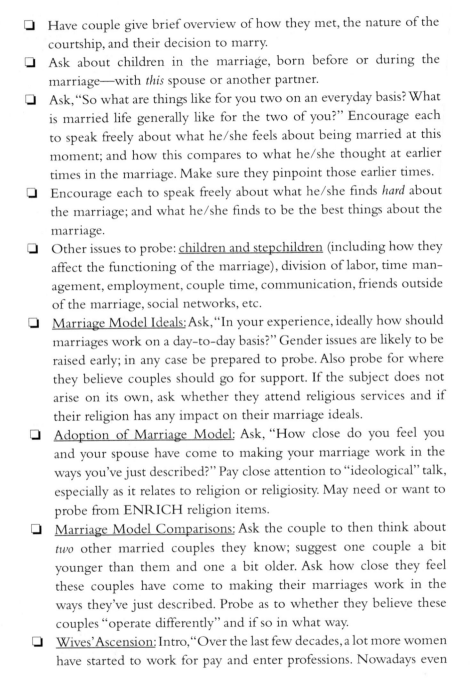

❏ Have couple give brief overview of how they met, the nature of the courtship, and their decision to marry.

❏ Ask about children in the marriage, born before or during the marriage—with *this* spouse or another partner.

❏ Ask, "So what are things like for you two on an everyday basis? What is married life generally like for the two of you?" Encourage each to speak freely about what he/she feels about being married at this moment; and how this compares to what he/she thought at earlier times in the marriage. Make sure they pinpoint those earlier times.

❏ Encourage each to speak freely about what he/she finds *hard* about the marriage; and what he/she finds to be the best things about the marriage.

❏ Other issues to probe: <u>children and stepchildren</u> (including how they affect the functioning of the marriage), division of labor, time management, employment, couple time, communication, friends outside of the marriage, social networks, etc.

❏ <u>Marriage Model Ideals:</u> Ask, "In your experience, ideally how should marriages work on a day-to-day basis?" Gender issues are likely to be raised early; in any case be prepared to probe. Also probe for where they believe couples should go for support. If the subject does not arise on its own, ask whether they attend religious services and if their religion has any impact on their marriage ideals.

❏ <u>Adoption of Marriage Model:</u> Ask, "How close do you feel you and your spouse have come to making your marriage work in the ways you've just described?" Pay close attention to "ideological" talk, especially as it relates to religion or religiosity. May need or want to probe from ENRICH religion items.

❏ <u>Marriage Model Comparisons:</u> Ask the couple to then think about *two* other married couples they know; suggest one couple a bit younger than them and one a bit older. Ask how close they feel these couples have come to making their marriages work in the ways they've just described. Probe as to whether they believe these couples "operate differently" and if so in what way.

❏ <u>Wives' Ascension:</u> Intro, "Over the last few decades, a lot more women have started to work for pay and enter professions. Nowadays even more women than men go to college. Which makes us wonder how these changes for women have led to changes in the relationships between husbands and wives. What do you think?"

For Black Couples: Follow up asking whether they have heard of and/or participated in discussions of black men having a difficult time in the job market, in school, in the legal system, etc. Probe how they might feel this is playing out in husband/wife relationships.

❏ Proximity to Whites: Intro, "There is a website/article about marriage that we have seen that quotes schoolchildren saying that 'marriage is for white people,' and we have had a number of friends and colleagues who have also seen this and commented on it. What do you make of such a statement?"

AUTHOR INDEX

SUBJECT INDEX